Daughters
of Tunis

Westview Case Studies in Anthropology
Series Editor: Edward F. Fischer
Vanderbilt University

Daughters of Tunis: Women, Family, and Networks in a Muslim City
Paula Holmes-Eber (University of Washington)

Tecpán Guatmala: A Modern Maya Town in Global and Local Context
Edward F. Fischer (Vanderbilt University) and
Carol Hendrickson (Marlboro College)

Fulbe Voices: Marriage, Islam, and Medicine in Northern Cameroon
Helen A. Regis (Louisiana State University)

FORTHCOMING:

The Lao: Gender, Power, and Livelihood
Carol Ireson-Doolittle (Willamette University) and
Geraldine Moreno-Black (University of Oregon)

Daughters of Tunis

Women, Family, and Networks
in a Muslim City

PAULA HOLMES-EBER
University of Washington

A Member of the Perseus Books Group

Copyright © 2003 by Westview Press, A Member of the Perseus Books Group

Westview Press books are available at special discounts for bulk purchases in the United States by corporations, institutions, and other organizations. For more information, please contact the Special Markets Department at the Perseus Books Group, 11 Cambridge Center, Cambridge MA 02142, or call (617) 252-5298 or e-mail special.markets@perseusbooks.com.

Published in 2003 in the United States of America by Westview Press, 5500 Central Avenue, Boulder, Colorado 80301–2877, and in the United Kingdom by Westview Press, 12 Hid's Copse Road, Cumnor Hill, Oxford OX2 9JJ

Find us on the World Wide Web at www.westviewpress.com

Library of Congress Cataloging-in-Publication Data
Holmes-Eber, Paula.
    Daughters of Tunis: women, family, and networks in a Muslim city / Paula Holmes-Eber.
        p.   cm.—(Westview case studies in anthropology)
    Includes bibliographical references and index.
    ISBN 0–8133–3943-X (HC: alk. paper)—0-8133-3944-8 (Pbk.)
    1. Women—Tunisia—Tunis—Social conditions.   2. Women—Tunisia—Tunis—Social life and customs.   3. Women—Social networks—Tunisia—Tunis.
4. Muslim women—Tunisia—Tunis.   5. Women in Islam—Tunisia—Tunis.
6. Ethnology—Tunisia—Tunis.   I. Title.   II. Series.
HQ1792.Z9 T855   2002
306'.099611—dc21

                                                                2002006168

The paper used in this publication meets the requirements of the American National Standard for Permanence of Paper for Printed Library Materials Z39.48–1984.

To Sherifa, Sarah, Amal, and Lilia

إخواتي توانسي

and for Anya, Yvonne, and Lorenz

my own survival network

Visit me once every year,
It's forbidden to forget me even once.
Visit me once every year,
It's unforgivable that you would forget one time—
Yes unforgivable!
That you could forget even once.

—Egyptian song by Derweech; sung by Fairouz
(Translation Paula Holmes-Eber)

Contents

Series Editor Preface

In the wake of the September 11, 2001 terrorist attacks on the World Trade Center and the Pentagon, America's attention turned dramatically to the Islamic world. The attacks had been carried out by Al Qaeda ("The Base"), a paramilitary organization dedicated to an extreme version of Islamic fundamentalism and based in Afghanistan. For many, the enemy seemed to be not just the few thousand armed Al Qaeda fighters but the whole of Islam; there was talk of a "clash of civilizations," and sweeping rhetoric bandied about "the Muslim world." But it is misleading to paint with such broad strokes. The real world is far too complex to boil down to a few neat categories: East and West, Christian and Muslim, right and wrong. It is just not that simple.

Ethnographers constantly struggle with this issue. How do we represent the great diversity of lived experience we are privileged to witness in a way that brings out broader significance without misrepresenting the people we have come to know as individuals? To address issues of social importance we must write broadly, but to base this on field data we must write very specifically. If one writes too specifically, interest in the subject will go no farther than the few other academics working in the same area; if one writes too broadly, data are distorted in what Kay Warren has called "death by abstraction."

Daughters of Tunis by Paula Holmes-Eber walks this fine line with lyric finesse. She introduces us to Muslim women in Tunis, taking us to the places where they live, work, and socialize: from private homes to public bath houses, from family weddings to outings at the beach.

Through her vivid narrative we can imagine ourselves as guests at a Tunisian house, tagging along as she goes visiting: the silver tray covered with sweets, pastries, and peeled mandarin oranges, accompanied by red or green tea and talk of the joys and hardships of life.

These visits and the conversations they engendered show us a "Muslim world" that resists a number of common presuppositions. First is the stereotype of Islamic countries as inherently sexist. In this regard, Tunisia, an Islamic nation with a history of pro-modernization policies, is quite progressive even by Western standards. Stated policy restricts use of traditional Muslim women's dress and encourages women to complete their education. And yet some women—even educated, middle-class women—*want* to wear the *hijab* (veil). This points to the shortcomings of another stereotype, that the gendered symbols associated with Islam (not only the *hijab* but also physical segregation and other restrictions) are inherently symbols of oppression. Take the case of Shedia, a university graduate and public school teacher, who was forbidden to wear a *hijab* at work. Her story reveals not only the rich complexity of life in Tunis but also the very nature of symbolic meaning. The genius of symbols rests in their malleability; their beauty (and significance) is truly in the eye of the beholder. For Shedia and other women like her, the *hijab* is an emblem of identity they are proud to display, a means of resistance against government policy, and is wrapped in unique webs of personal and social meanings.

In some ways Tunisian women are caught between the more egalitarian stance of the state and the more traditional expectations of their families. For many men, having their wives work outside the house is a sign of disgrace. I am not sure how uniquely Islamic or Tunisian this is—such conflict would not be out of place in a John Cheever story or my field notes from the Maya area—but it does point to the disconnect between women's desires and culturally validated male intentions. Attitudes toward marriage and dating reflect similar conflicts. For example, Holmes-Eber introduces us to Najet, a young woman torn between her more libertarian values and her parents' enforcement of their traditionalist views. Najet's parents will not let her marry her illicit boyfriend, but, as she has already enjoyed the pleasures of his bed, she fears that she will be considered unfit to marry anyone else and thus be denied the security and comfort of a family of her own. Holmes-Eber convincingly shows that even women such as Najet are part of social networks that create a strong sense of community for Tunisian women. On average, women visit seventeen households on a regular basis. Most of these are visits to family, the wife's relative as well as the husband's (challenging a strict patriarchal view of Islamic kinship). Other visits are to neighbors who provide an important social security network, especially for immigrants to the city. Holmes-Eber shows how these fluid networks are created and maintained through practice. In doing so, she reveals the micro-politics of everyday life: deciding whom to visit, following the unspoken rules of economic exchange, and negotiating relative status through gifts.

The series Westview Case Studies in Anthropology recognizes the peoples we study as active agents enmeshed in global as well as local systems of politics, economics, and cultural flows. Tunis (population 3 million) has long been a globalized city; during the roaring 1920s almost half its population was foreign born. Today it retains this cosmopolitan flair, and Holmes-Eber artfully shows the unique synthesis of Western modernity and traditional custom that is constantly being worked out through concrete social networks. In so doing, she advances the overarching goal of this series, which is to impart an empathetic understanding of alternative ways of viewing and acting in the world as well as a solid basis for critical thought regarding the culturally contingent nature of knowledge.

Edward F. Fischer

Preface

This book began initially as an ethnographic study of women, family, and development in Tunis. In its first incarnation, I intended to present a scholarly study of women and their families in Tunisia, a country that despite its radical modernization policies had received scant academic attention in the English-speaking world.

At about the time I began my first drafts, however, I had been teaching several years of both introductory classes in anthropology and upper-level seminars on the Middle East and North Africa. Given the immense and growing literature on Middle Eastern and Muslim women, I had initially assumed that I would have no difficulty in finding suitable ethnographies that provided excellent scholarship while offering students a solid introduction to many of the social, economic, and cultural issues facing women of the region today. To my surprise, however, I found myself constantly changing my reading list each time a new quarter started: Some of the books, although offering excellent research, were too dense and technical; others focused on a limited category of women such as the urban poor or a small rural community, hence failing to provide the comparative perspective necessary to understand the range of women's experiences. Although the number of commendable recent readers on women in the Muslim world did offer the breadth and analysis of contemporary issues that I sought, I still longed for an in-depth ethnographic study that could provide the holistic context and qualitative perspective that students in my classes desperately needed.

Thus was born *Daughters of Tunis,* a readable, intimate, yet theoretically solid book that could synthesize the best of both detailed ethnographic anthropological fieldwork and comparative quantitative analysis. My research on networks fell naturally into the structure of a book not only relevant to Middle Eastern scholars but also appropriate for classrooms. Since networks create the essential underlying fabric of daily life in Tunisia, it was logical, indeed imperative, that I cover such topics as marriage, family, and kinship (Chapters 4 and 5); gender roles (Chapter 2); religion (Chapter 7); local economies and development (Chapter 6); migration and community formation (Chapters 4 and 5); social exchange and status (Chapters 3 and 7); and class, language, and political and social structure (Chapter 7).

Supporting front and back material also provides supplementary information on such topics as the cultural role of language ("Notes on Language Use and Transliteration of Tunisian Arabic"), Arab kinship systems and terminology ("Glossary of Tunisian Kinship Terms"), and research methodology ("Appendix 1: The Survey"). To make the text easily readable while retaining the quantitative and theoretical strength of the research, the statistical results of my research have been presented in tables in Appendix 2. Likewise, relevant research and suggestions for further reading are provided in endnotes and in a brief discussion preceding the References section.

Influenced by postmodernist concerns about ethnographic representation as well as my own interest in research methodology, I decided consciously to insert the ethnographer into the ethnography, creating a vivid image of the fieldwork process while challenging the reader to separate research from the researcher.

Yet this book is not just stories—a tenuous line between literature and anthropology. It is built firmly on the notion that data can be quantified (as long as one is aware of the assumptions behind the quantities). *Daughters of Tunis* is perhaps sometimes an uneasy marriage between both quantitative and qualitative approaches. And yet I believe that by merging the two, somewhere in that strange intersection between numbers and stories, between fact and fiction, lies the reality of women's lives in Tunisia. It is my hope that the reader, by moving between the intimate details of women's individual stories and the anonymous aggregate numbers of a replicable and comparative survey, can develop a concrete picture of the struggles that Tunisian women and their families are facing while also placing this information in a larger context, examining the effects that social and economic factors have on women's options and strategies, not only in Tunis but throughout the Middle East and the developing world.

Paula Holmes-Eber
Bainbridge Island, Washington

Acknowledgments

With many thanks to:

Lorenz Eber, my husband and photographer
Deborah Wheeler, friend, colleague, and critical reader
    of many versions
Karl Yambert, my patient and persistent editor
Jean Mrad and CEMAT in Tunis, for their library, office space,
    and years of practical assistance
Muhammed Eissa, for songs and Arabic interpretations
Helen Schwartzman, Karen Hansen, Oswald Werner, and Robert
    Launay, my first scholarly commentators
Laurence Michelak and Georges Sabagh, for conferences and
    many discussions about North African migrants
Mark Tessler, for promoting early versions of this book
Terri deYoung and Philip Schuyler, for advice on Arabic lyrics
Keith Walters, for suggestions on Tunisian Arabic transliteration
Richard Lobban, for assistance with maps
Dee Mortensen and Bridget Julian, for feedback on revisions
The Middle East Center at the University of Washington
The Fulbright Program
The American Institute of Maghribi Studies, for travel and
    conference expenses
USIS in Tunis and Bob Krill, for practical support in the field

My anonymous reviewers, for detailed and insightful comments
And the women of Tunis: who opened their hearts, their homes, and
their lives to a strange American with a hilarious accent and lots
of questions.

P. H.E.

Notes on Language Use and Transliteration of Tunisian Arabic

Transliterating Tunisian Arabic poses a number of problems. First, since the Tunisian Arabic dialect is spoken, not written, there is no consensus among scholars or Tunisians themselves as to a consistent Arabic transliteration system. Although Tunisia is a small country, there is considerable dialectical variation from region to region. This variation is magnified in the capital city of Tunis, where I conducted my research. There is a *Tunisoise* dialect that is spoken by the original Tunis inhabitants and approximated by upwardly mobile migrants. But owing to the rapid influx of migrants, not only from Tunisia but also from neighboring countries, there is no one consistent dialect spoken in the city.

Second, Tunisian Arabic is far from a static language. Owing to Tunisia's contact with many foreign rulers, as well as an indigenous Berber-speaking population, the language has absorbed numerous words, expressions, and grammatical forms that have non-Arabic origins. In recent years, contact with the French has resulted in the ongoing incorporation of many French words—particularly among the upper classes and bourgeoisie—often resulting in some most interesting amalgamations of French and Arabic. It took me several months of fieldwork, for example, to realize that the word *sarabis* was an Arabized plural for the French word *service* or tea service.

Finally, and perhaps most challenging, is the fact that Tunisians as individuals do not speak one consistent language. Since language is an important indicator of social status and affiliation, Tunisians adjust their language according to the person being addressed. Depending on the context, speakers will slip comfortably between the dialect of their region of origin, a more standardized "educated" Arabic, French, and/or Arabized French, often within the span of a few sentences.

How, then, does one accurately represent the language spoken and heard during my interviews? For the sake of consistency (and the sanity of my readers), in this study I have elected to select one standardized transliteration of each word, based on its most common pronunciation. Thus, rather than represent the exact dialectical nuances of pronunciation that would result, for example, in the word "home" being transliterated variously as *beet, bait, baat,* or *bit,* I have elected to use the single transliteration *beet* for all interviews, since this transliteration would be most readily understood by most Tunisians.

To make the transliterations intelligible to Arabic scholars, I have, wherever possible, adopted the system proposed by the *International Journal of Middle East Studies.* Arabic words that have become standardized in the literature (e.g., Ramadan) conform to accepted spellings. Since it is also my desire to provide the reader with an authentic sense of social life and interaction, as well as to create a representative document for native speakers themselves, I have included a number of transliterations, particularly of vowels, and word ellisions, that offer a more accurate sense of the actual language spoken in my interviews.[1]

Finally, to make the book accessible to a more general readership, the emphatic consonants ص ط ظ ح as well as ذ have been transliterated into their closest English-language approximations instead of using more cumbersome phonetic conventions. A full explanation of the transliteration system is available on the supporting website for this book.

Note

1. The systems used by Ben Abdelkader et al. (1977) and Webber (1991) serve as the basis for these linguistic interpretations.

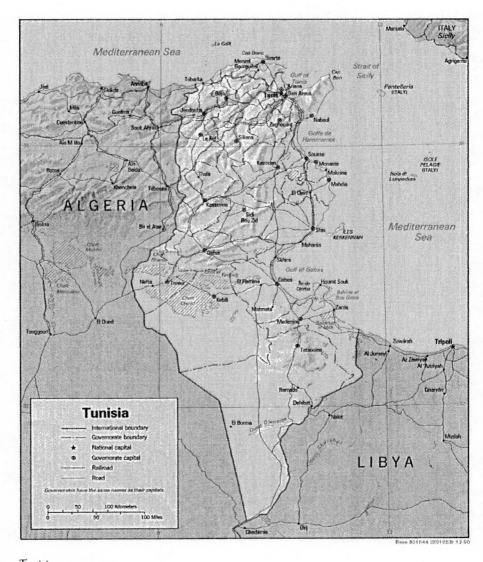

Tunisia

I

Introduction

Lush-dark-haired and brown-eyed, twenty-seven-year-old Hannan,[1] her pregnant belly gently nudging the stomach of her neatly tailored dress and jacket, leans forward to pour the steaming minted green tea into my glass. A university graduate, Hannan has just returned from another long day at the British Embassy in Tunis, where she works as a multilingual translator. She and her husband, a successful banker, live alone in a newly constructed apartment building on the outskirts of the capital of Tunisia, spending weekends and evenings entertaining their friends from the university or driving in their car to visit Hannan's extended family, who live eighty kilometers away. I have stopped by to visit, to ask Hannan for some help with my survey, and to catch up on the latest news about Hannan's family and work.

"Aq'ad, aq'ad" (Sit, sit). Voluble, dancing-eyed, forty-three-year-old Nura pats a spot for me in between the many brown-skinned, shouting children of her eight neighbors, all sprawled in colorful patterned skirts and brightly decorated head scarves on woven wool blankets on the beach. A housewife with less than six years of schooling, Nura spends most of her days in the courtyard of a once-elegant Arab house in the old city or *medina* of Tunis, cooking, washing, chatting, arguing, and sharing her joys and sorrows with her children, her mother-in-law,

1

brother-in-law, and the other eight neighbors who rent rooms around the now-dilapidated courtyard. It is another gasping-hot July day, and so, their baskets overflowing with *kaskrout* (Tunisian sandwiches), sodas, peanuts, and *bonbons*, Nura and her neighbors have settled down on the warm yellow sands of the Le Marsa beach to laugh, exchange stories, wipe off children's noses, and dry wet, sandy feet on a long-anticipated day's outing together.

Tired and wan, almost disappearing into her thin, pale, cotton dress, Miriam scrubs the last of the white-and-green-tiled countertops in the modern kitchen of Madame Al Mohad's beautiful orange-tree-gardened villa. A twenty-eight-year-old maid from Hamma in the south of Tunisia, Miriam lives in a shack with electricity but no running water near the dusty railroad tracks of a billowing smoke-stacked industrial section of Tunis. She shares the squatter home with her sickly husband Sami, who works sporadically in construction, and Sami's teenage sister, who takes care of their nine-month-old baby, while Miriam cleans Madame's house to support them. Wiping off her hands on her apron, Miriam smiles shyly as she pulls out a stool to sit for a moment and chat with me among the piles of purple satins and black velvets in Madame Al Mohad's sewing room.

"Bchir, don't get dirty," Sherifa's *louza* (sister-in-law) Kareema shouts as tousle-haired, four-year-old Bchir trundles off munching on a sticky handful of sugared almonds. "Kareema is like a sister to me," tall, slender, twenty-six-year-old Sherifa smiles, offering me a brown paper-wrapped cone of nuts. "We love each other. We are always together," Kareema adds. Six years ago, Sherifa dropped out of high school to marry the man she loved, Kareema's adopted brother. Although he was a well-to-do landed farmer from an old Tunis family, Sherifa's family had hoped she would marry her paternal cousin. Her father's relatives did not forgive her and refuse to visit her now. Yet Sherifa still spends her life in a world of kin. Sharing cooking, shopping, child care, and errands, she goes everywhere with her four sisters-in-law, who live in houses built next door to one another. Sherifa and Kareema spend their days and nights together, drinking tea, eating nuts, and shouting after each other's children.

Working women and stay-at-home mothers, university graduates and illiterate wives, migrants to the city and women from old-established Tunis families, well-to-do or barely making ends meet, these women are all part of the new generation of Muslim women in Tunisia. Born into a rapidly developing nation, facing not only radical economic and social change but also astonishing legal reforms for Muslim women, Hannan, Nura, Miriam, and Sherifa are daughters of a new Tunis. These women live in a world radically different from that of their mothers: a world that only a few decades ago was primarily rural and agricultural and now is predominantly industrial and urbanized; a world in which Muslim women may hold jobs in factories or the government, go to school, vote, choose their own husbands, walk the streets without veils, initiate divorce, and live in their own households, separate and sometimes far away from their in-laws.

At the vanguard of legal and social reform for Muslim women, Tunisia is the obvious choice for a study of the impact of development and social change on women and their families—not only within the Middle East and Muslim world—but in all developing nations where men and women are willingly or unwillingly being thrust rapidly into the global economy; where women's rights and roles are being relegislated, often uneasily clashing with existing cultural beliefs and norms; and where extended families are scrambling to adjust to the impact of migration and urbanization on traditional household structures.

How is this new generation of women coping with such rapid and unprecedented changes? What is the impact of education, employment, migration, and changing marriage rights on women's personal and economic options or their roles and relations with their families? Has development had similar effects on women of different classes or regions of origin? And how have women reconciled Muslim and Arab beliefs regarding gender roles and marriage with the current realities of men and women working and studying together? In this book I seek to answer some of these questions by offering an intimate look at the daily lives and survival strategies of more than sixty Muslim women and their households whom I interviewed, observed, and surveyed in Tunis from 1986 to 1987 and again in 1993.[2]

WOMEN, FAMILY, AND SOCIAL CHANGE IN TUNISIA

Tunisia's independence from the French in 1956 marked the beginning of a rapid shift from a primarily rural and agriculturally based economy to the current highly urbanized (more than half of the population of the country now lives in the capital city of Tunis) and industrial society that is entering the new millennium. Led by the late president Bourguiba (who ruled from 1956 to 1987), an aggressively pro-Western and pro-development program was initiated, instituting numerous reforms designed to make the nation competitive in the world market economy.

One of the first and most significant pieces of legislation enacted by the Bourguiban government was the Personal Status Code. This code continues to be one of the most radical and liberal sets of laws on women and the family in the Arab and Muslim world today, granting women numerous rights and protections paralleled by few Middle Eastern countries (with the exception perhaps of Turkey). The Personal Status Code granted women citizenship and the right to vote, forbade the veil, abolished polygyny, improved women's rights in divorce, and challenged the practice of arranged marriages. Women's education and employment were also encouraged; free schooling at all levels through the university was offered to both women and men. And further laws were decreed encouraging women's employment through protection of their rights in the workplace.

Women's rights continued to be expanded by Bourguiba's successor, Ben Ali. Women were granted more privileges in divorce and custody cases, and labor laws were revised to remove earlier restrictions on women's salary and to prevent job discrimination.

Alarmed by these revolutionary new laws, in the years after Tunisia's independence researchers began linking the changing social status of women and new family status laws to disruptions in the "traditional" patriarchal extended Tunisian family. Studies documented the gradual disappearance of the extended Arab household, increasing divorce and tensions in the marital dyad, erosion of patriarchal authority and consequent parent-child conflict, the rupture of relations with absent/migrant parents, and a decrease in arranged marriages. Other studies across the Maghreb found similar crises in parent-child relations due to emigration, as well as an increase in sexual freedom prior to marriage and greater choice in mate selection.

In addition to legislation concerning women's rights, the Bourguiban government began a number of progressive economic programs designed to promote industry and Tunisian economic self-sufficiency. After an initial failed move toward socialism, which divided up the large, protected *habous* lands of wealthy families and the French *colons*, the Bourguiban regime moved toward a protectionist model of a free market industrial economy, maintaining strict controls on prices, importation, and investment. Policies promoting heavy investment in industry and tourism finally paid off by the end of the 1980s. The spectacular sandy beaches and coasts of Tunisia (particularly from Nabeul to Mahdia and on the island of Jerba) soon became lined with row after row of large, white washed Tunisian-style two-to five-star hotels designed to attract vacationing Europeans, many of whom brought their own radically different customs of topless sunbathing and "loose" sexual behavior. And Tunisia began manufacturing everything from clothing to plastic tubs to pottery to batteries, much of it for the nation's own consumption. Thirty years after independence only 13 percent of Tunisia's gross national product (GNP) came from agriculture, whereas 45 percent derived from industry and 42 percent from services—predominantly tourism (Samuelson 1990). Considering that Tunisia is one of the few Arab nations with only a few natural resources (primarily phosphates), this accomplishment is no small feat.

Yet the fairy-tale story has had its downside: several years of rampant inflation in the 1980s; food riots due to price controls on bread and other essentials; increasing international debts; and, reflecting the dissatisfaction of some with the overly liberal laws regarding women and the bizarre contrasts of nudist European sunbathers with Muslim

Coastline north of Tunis.

notions of modesty, a series of Islamist group protests, arrests, and bombings.

In November 1987 the prime minister, Ben Ali, quietly and quickly overthrew the ailing and senile President Bourguiba. Under Ben Ali's leadership Tunisia then instituted an aggressive structural adjustment program with the guidance of the International Monetary Fund (IMF).[3] In recent years, the country has become a model of success for the IMF, citing reduced inflation, a lowered deficit, and a consistent gross domestic product (GDP) growth of 4.2 percent per year (*Tunisia Digest* 1992, 1993). Tunisia's continued high unemployment rate, which varied between 15 and 16 percent in the mid-1990s—a reflection of the economy's difficulty in keeping pace with the growing workforce—has, however, drawn criticism as well as praise (*North Africa Journal* 1998 and ABC News 1999).

Although some have benefited from these new economic and social changes, the gains have not been distributed evenly. As the growing educated middle class of government employees and permanent factory management has received secure positions with reliable and good salaries, the uneducated and unskilled have been left behind to fend for themselves. Manual laborers face serious underemployment, with unpredictable and sporadic work and income. Self-employment is widespread, with both men and women running formal and informal businesses. Tiny "hole-in-the wall" stores selling baguettes, tobacco, and toothpaste proliferate alongside businesses offering moped repair, used plumbing and auto parts, traditional pottery, and handmade shoes. Women, although not always visible on the streets, run hairdressing salons from their homes, sew clothes on commission for their relatives, and make handmade knitted goods for sale in the *souks* (traditional markets).

Although the Tunisian government does require that large firms provide health insurance, disability, and old-age pensions, these social security programs tend to apply to a small privileged minority of stably employed persons in government and large industries—the social class that, in general, is least in need of assistance. Also, like many other Muslim countries, Tunisia has no comprehensive social assistance or welfare programs for the poor or disabled, assuming that the religious practice of *zakat* or almsgiving is adequate.

As a result, women—who typically leave the workforce after marriage and/or often work in the informal sector as maids, in handicrafts production, or in agriculture—generally fall through the gaps in these programs, as does the large male population of the irregularly and self-employed. For these men and women, death, illness, disability, the failure of one's small business, and unemployment are feared financial catastrophes that can, in a few minutes, leave an entire household destitute.

HOUSEHOLDS, DEVELOPMENT, AND WOMEN'S SURVIVAL NETWORKS

Despite the immense opportunity to analyze the rapid effects of pro-Western development on women in a Muslim country, disappointingly, only limited information is available in English on women in Tunisia. Most of the available research in English has focused primarily on the ideology of change—for example, studies documenting Tunisian legal reforms, or men's and women's attitudes and political responses toward these reforms.[4]

Although publications in French and Arabic on women and the family in Tunisia have been more extensive, like the available English-language literature, this research tends to examine ideological issues such as legislation affecting women, women's movements, and cultural ideologies regarding women or to focus on statistical trends such as women's employment, health, and education,[5] rather than analyzing the actual impact of these changes on the day-to-day lives and experiences of women in Tunisia. Only a handful of studies[6] examine in any detail the specific negotiations, strategies, and choices employed by Tunisian women and their families in adapting to social and economic change.

This neglect of research at the micro level of the household and the individual in large part reflects a general bias in the development literature toward a "top-down" analysis of development and social change—an approach that assumes that governments rather than individuals effect change. As Hatem (1999) observes, although there have been a variety of narratives over the past century discussing modernization, gender, and the family in the Middle East, almost all discourses have viewed the state as the primary agent of development and social change. These narratives place the state and modernization in conflict with what is viewed as the traditional/Muslim family, which is blamed for women's oppressed position and lack of integration into the formal economy.

In contrast to this "top-down" approach, a burgeoning ethnographic literature on women in the Middle East and in other developing areas— particularly Latin America and the Caribbean—suggests that men, women, and households are not simply passive recipients of change but rather active agents, who define and reshape the outcome of change according to their own needs and perceptions. White (1994), Early (1993a, 1993b), Hoodfar (1997, 1990), Lobban (1998b), and Singerman (1994) have described Middle Eastern women's many enterprising solutions to their new social and economic conditions, including the sale and exchange of domestic skills like laundry washing, cooking, and handwork; the creation of informal savings associations as a buffer against economic instability and a means to obtain luxury goods; and the development of social and political networks that allow women to navigate the seemingly impossible bureaucracy and red tape of health care and social service programs.

An open air market.

Recognition of women's participation in the informal economy has resulted in an explosion of research on women's direct or indirect economic contributions to the household through their domestic "home work." Yet in most developing countries (and for that matter, the developed world), many other long-term economic services such as education, health care, and social insurance and assistance also continue to be the responsibility of households and, in particular, women.

Perhaps one of the least understood economic and political domestic tasks that women and households perform are what di Leonardo (1987) describes as "kin work" and Papanek (1979) as "family status production." This work, simply defined, consists of those tasks—letters, visits, gift exchanges, attendance at ritual events, and so forth—conducted to maintain and expand social ties with kin, work colleagues, or other socially advantageous contacts. Although women's networking has no immediate tangible economic consequences for the family, as does, say, a husband's paycheck, ultimately this work is critical for the household's survival: creating networks that provide insurance against economic and personal calamities, as well as emotional and practical support, services, and access to jobs, goods, and information.

Research in Latin America as well as recent analyses in the Middle East all point to the important and central roles these networks play in women's survival strategies: the rational choices and options women utilize to cope in often unstable and changing social and economic environments.[7] Almost all of these studies, however, have focused on the urban poor, the social category that is, in general, benefiting least from development.

As Young and Shami (1997) point out, cross-class comparisons—and especially investigations of the newly developing middle classes—are seriously lacking in studies of women and families in the Middle East. Given the mounting evidence that development is far from even, with significantly different effects on men, women, and households of varying socioeconomic levels, it is clear that to understand the choices and actions made by women and their households, we need to account for the economic and social differences *between* women in the Middle East. In this book, I examine the ways in which Tunisian women's household incomes, educational levels, current and past employment, and social class and region of origin influence the kinds of survival networks they rely on to cope in one of the fastest industrializing and urbanizing nations in the Third World.

THE STUDY

Most studies of women and development present either analyses of general statistical patterns—a macro perspective—or detailed, in-depth micro-level studies of women in a specific community. This research, in contrast, offers both. Using a unique analysis that combines intimate and personal stories of women such as Hannan, Nura, Miriam, and Sherifa with a detailed statistical survey of women's networks and social resources, this study permits not only an understanding of the "complexity of individual lives" (Abu Lughod 1993) but also a statistically comparative and replicable interpretation of the personal, social, and economic options available to women of different socioeconomic backgrounds.

My research employs a network analysis approach to understanding and tracing the links between women and households. The primary orienting notion of network analysis is its view of the individual as embedded in a network of relations or social links with others, explaining social acts in terms of the structure and nature of relations among actors. There are two distinct but complementary modes of network analysis: those that examine the structure or morphology of social networks—a *structural* perspective—and those that examine the content or nature of the links in networks—a transactional or *interactionist* perspective. This ethnography reflects this latter, interactionist approach, focusing on who is in the woman's network, the kinds of interactions (visiting, exchange of food, child care, etc.) that represent network participation, the frequency of women's visits, and the nature of exchanges. Since stage in the life cycle and marital status may have a significant impact on network composition, this study focuses on married women with unmarried children living at home. This age group (approximately twenty to forty-five) represents the first adult generation of women to have grown up during and after Tunisia's independence: the first generation of women to benefit from and struggle with the extraordinary changes in women's education, employment, and new legal and marital rights of the past forty years.

To understand women's networks and relationships, I became an active participant in seven distinct and separate communities throughout the greater Tunis area (the *medina,* the *villeneuve,* the *lotissements,* the wealthy *menzehs,* two suburbs, and a semirural community on the fringes of the city). In total, I completed more than a year of participant observation of women's daily social activities in twenty-four separate households during my first year in Tunis (September 1986–August 1987) and an additional fifty-two hours of observation during my follow-up trip in June 1993. In addition to my observations of women's network activities, I conducted twenty formal, taped interviews in French and Arabic with Tunisian women and their male relatives met through my social networks.

To obtain a comparative cross-sample of women's networks, I also undertook a survey of thirty-six women on the beaches of Tunis. In Tunisia, beaches are among the few open spaces where women can socialize with "outsiders" without fear of criticism. Local beaches—those frequented by Tunisians rather than tourists—are not generally used for suntanning or meeting the opposite sex as in Europe or the United States. Many of the more conservative Tunisian women do not even wear bathing suits or other revealing clothing, preferring to swim in an old dress that modestly covers the body. Instead, a trip to the beach is considered a family activity where women, their children, and kin go to socialize and escape the heat of the city. Since going to the beach is generally a daylong social affair, women had the time and leisure to talk to me freely at length for my survey interviews. In return, I would socialize and tell stories about the United States, the only payment the women would accept.

Although the survey is small (and not appropriate for large descriptive statistics about the general Tunis population), the sample size is perfectly appropriate for a statistical study of the relationships *between* variables (for example, the effects of women's education, income, and migration on networks) using inferential statistics such as regression, ANOVA, and *t*-tests. A complete description of the survey sample is included in Appendix 1.

In the following chapters I illustrate how Tunisian women and their households respond to and cope with the new industrial, urban environment, insuring themselves against the calamities of life by investing in cooperative networks with kin, neighbors, and friends. Chapter 2 introduces the cultural and spatial context of women's networks in a Muslim society and questions some of our assumptions about the "privacy" of women's domestic space. In Chapter 3 I discuss the important relationships among social status, visiting patterns, and ties of exchange and reciprocity for women in Tunis.

Chapters 4–7 then focus on the specific network styles of women in the study. Using the cases of Miriam, Sherifa, Nura, and Hannan, I analyze how women's varying income, education, and migration influence the three network patterns evident in my study: the "kin exclusive network," the "neighbor network," and the "friendship pattern." Miriam's story in Chapter 4 describes the continuing importance of kinship, the central role of marriage, and the intriguing problems of mate selection for Tunisian women today. Sherifa's street in Chapter 5 serves as the entry for challenging some of the prevailing assumptions in the literature regarding the patrilinearity of kinship and the impact of migration on household structure and family ties. In Chapter 6 I examine the role that neighborhood networks play in the daily and long-term survival of poor migrant *baldi* women such as Nura. And finally, Hannan's friendship pattern in Chapter 7 illustrates the ways in which women's religious holidays and celebrations reflect and perpetuate class and social status boundaries in an increasingly socially mobile society.

Notes

1. To protect the identity of the people in this study, all personal names and some place-names or other identifying information have been altered.
2. I would like to express my thanks for the support received during my field visits from a Fulbright grant (1986–1987) and travel funds from the American Institute of Maghribi studies (1993).
3. He also began a severe and repressive attack on Islamist groups, accompanied by reports of torture, beatings, and death, which have placed the country on Amnesty International's Human Rights violator's lists (Brand 1998).
4. See, e.g., Brand (1998); Galal (1995); Tessler, Rogers, and Schneider (1978); and Zamiti-Horchani (1986) for English-language literature on women in Tunisia.
5. See, e.g., Bourquia, Charrad, and Gallagher (1996, v. 2); Chamari (1990); Labidi (1987, 1989); Ferchiou (1996); Bernard (1990); L. Taamallah (1982, 1981); M. Taamallah (1986, 1990); Zouari-Bouattour (1996); and Republique Tunisienne (1988) for the more extensive French- and Arabic-language literature on Tunisian women.
6. See, e.g., Dorra Mahfoudh-Draoui's (1993) ethnography of rural women; Malika Zamiti-Horchani's (1997) research on wives of migrant workers; and the recent work by Ferchiou (1998), Lobban (1998b), and Berry-Chikahoui (1998) on Tunisian women's participation in the invisible economy of Tunisia.
7. For research on survival strategies, see Lomnitz (1977), Chant (1991), and Gonzales de la Rocha (1994) as well as recent analyses on the Middle East by Hoodfar (1997, 1990, 1996) and Singerman (1995, 1996).

City of Tunis

2

Men's and Women's Spaces in Tunis

"What's important here is, you know, to be always in the house with friends or the family," lush-brown-eyed, twenty-seven-year-old Hannan explains to me earnestly, leaning over the neat piles of letters in French, Arabic, and English on her desk in the British Embassy. She carefully peels the wrinkled skin from a tangerine in her hand, dessert for the lunch of spicy *harissa*-filled Tunisian sandwiches we have been sharing in her office, and offers me a piece as she continues, "People, they don't go out on Saturday nights, but they stay at home, and they have people who would come and, you know, stay and talk and—like a family party. Just sit and talk and drink tea and eat sunflower seeds or peanuts or things like that and just be together—sometimes listening to the TV until one o'clock."

I lay down my pen to finish the tangerine, which is now stickily dripping onto my field notes, figuring that since the interview is being taped, I can afford to miss a few notes. Hannan smiles. Accustomed by now to informal American table manners after a year of studying with Americans at the University in London and three years of working for the British Embassy, she hands me a napkin, adding, "So it's more to be in the house than outside because outside you can't find anything, you can't do anything."

Social life for Muslim women in Tunis does not occur in outdoor spaces such as restaurants, movie theaters, shopping malls, or parks, although the capital of Tunisia, like most major cities, has a growing number of these amenities. It takes place in the home. The domestic domain in Tunis, however, is not a "private haven" or "prison"[1] where Muslim women are secluded from the important political and economic activities of the "real world." On the contrary, the "happening" place to be is inside the home: sitting and talking and drinking tea and eating sunflower seeds and peanuts and visiting with one's friends and family. Indeed, in Hannan's opinion, it is the external world that is empty and lacking, for "outside you can't find anything, you can't do anything."

Although Hannan would appear to be the ideal example of the "modernized" Tunisian woman—highly educated, employed outside of the home, and dressed in Western clothing—like all of the women I interviewed, she still continues to view her social world within existing Arab and Muslim cultural conceptions of male and female spaces. Abu Lughod (1985) suggests that we should view the separation of men and women in Muslim society as a division into two "separate worlds" where men and women live and act in parallel but distinct social realms with their own rules, opportunities, and hierarchies. Women's space centers on the lively, bustling, political domestic domain.

Tunisian women's homes are noisy, active, busy social centers, filled with neighbors who have dropped in ostensibly to borrow tea; friends who have stopped by to drop off the magazines they had promised during the last week; and relatives who live in the house, next door, upstairs, or are visiting for a few weeks. The courtyard or enclosed garden of the home is not only a center of domestic activities such as drying foods and washing clothes but also the place where most major social celebrations such as circumcision parties, engagements, and weddings continue to be held. (Although there is a new trend among the aspiring middle and upper classes to hold some of these celebrations in rented halls or *salas*.)

Hannan's conceptualization of the home as an important "public" and "social" space lies in sharp contrast to classic American ideologies that have portrayed the home as a "private" retreat distinctly separate from the public economic and political domain. Although both U.S. and Middle Eastern cultures equate women with the domestic domain and

Two university students look down upon the medina.

men with the outside world, the meaning and experience of women's domestic lives does not necessarily translate cross-culturally. Indeed, privacy, in the American sense of being left alone without human contact, is an alien concept in Arab culture. Most of Arab daily life centers around close intimate human contact; in fact, a Westerner's desire to be alone is often seen as antisocial, cold, rude, and even abnormal.

Tunisian views of the home as a "public" social space led to much frustration and confusion for me during my early months of fieldwork in Tunis. Whereas I saw my home as a place to retreat from my fieldwork, gather my thoughts, and have some time to myself, my friends assumed that—because I was home—I most certainly would be delighted to receive a visit and have some company. This was especially true on weekends and Sundays, which are the typical visiting days in the week. Halfway through my fieldwork I finally came to a rather ironic solution to finding time alone. When we needed some peace of mind, my husband and I would leave our bustling social life of the "private" home to spend the day outdoors, in the anonymous and impersonal "public" spaces of the city parks, boulevards, and restaurants—or even go to the noisy but still not personally demanding social world of the *souks* or markets.

Even though the home is the center of much social life for both men and women in Tunis, there is no question that it is primarily a female space. Although men do participate in major home celebrations such as weddings or formal visits, much of their social and free time is spent away from the home, at work, in cafés, and—especially for the unemployed youth—on street corners. Particularly for older men and teenagers, the home is primarily a space to sleep, eat, and interact with their immediate family.

Whereas during visits I would remain in the women's homes drinking tea or helping in the kitchen, after a quick greeting and maybe a socially appropriate gulping down of a glass of tea or coffee, my husband Lorenz would be escorted off unannounced to a local café; for a visit to another male friend; or to check out the latest problem with the car, the moped, or (in more recent years) the computer. Even when he would remain in the house, male and female groupings often quickly formed, with each group moving to a separate space within the room or house.

Just as men go through numerous subtle but important symbolic and physical activities to avoid trespassing on women's domestic space, so too are women expected to follow socially accepted rules to avoid intruding on men's space outside of the home.

MOVING INTO AND OUT OF MEN'S SPACES

The division between female and male spaces in the Muslim world might best be described as paralleling the distinction between family/friend and outsider/foe. The Arab Muslim woman's world consists primarily of kin and close family friends, whereas men hold the responsibility for interacting with outsiders. Thus when women in Tunis move outside in the male domain, they are generally accompanied by an escort, preferably a male relative who will defend their honor and assist in conducting transactions with strangers. Similarly, when a stranger comes to the house, a male relative is expected to meet him or her; a woman alone might refuse to come to the door or to permit the person into the home.

Perhaps one of the first indications that Tunisian women do not circulate freely outdoors is their extreme reluctance to go out alone, partic-

Transportation takes many forms on the streets of Tunis.

ularly when the errand is not absolutely necessary. For example, I have recorded only one instance in my diary when a female friend (an unmarried student) came to visit me unaccompanied by either a male relative (preferred pattern), female relative, or girlfriend. In contrast, my husband's male friends almost always came alone when visiting.

In cases where women must go out unescorted, the most protected forms of transportation—either their own car or a taxi (buses are used only as a last resort)—are selected if they can afford it. The importance of having an escort, or at least a car, is illustrated by the following conversation with Mounia, a forty-one-year-old widow, whose three children were still too young to be considered serious escorts.

"Do you ever go out in the evenings or on Sundays?" I asked in an interview in Mounia's comfortable villa one afternoon.

"Sundays, not always," she replied in Arabic. "When my husband was alive I'd go out, but now, never."

Mounia's close friend, who had come over to visit when she heard about the interview added, "Before, she always went out. Now because of a car—she doesn't have one—that's why. If she had a car she'd go out."

Traveling with an intermediary (an escort) is one way to prevent un-acceptable intrusion into the male domain; a second method is through covering the body, either completely with a white sheet, called a *sifsaree*, or through wearing a head veil (*hijab*) and long dress (an outfit gener-ally associated with conservative Islamic groups). Because of former President Bourgiba's edicts against veiling, the *sifsaree* is primarily seen only on older women or women from rural areas. Most younger women wear European-style clothing or colorful, long gowns called *jalebas*.

During my first field trip to Tunisia in 1986–1987 the *hijab* had been rapidly making an appearance, especially on university women. MacLeod (1991) and Hessini (1994) argue that the veil's return among educated and working women in the Middle East is a response to new sexual pressures resulting from their entrance into the workforce and educational system. By donning the veil these women make a statement to men that they are honorable women, who have entered the male space purely for the purpose of education or employment.

In my later trips to Tunis (1993, 1994) the *hijab* was facing an interest-ing turnabout, as illustrated by the case of Shedia, a married, university-educated high school teacher. She was a devout Muslim who had decided to wear the *hijab* while she was studying at the University of Tunis. In contrast, neither her sister Latifa nor her mother wore the *hijab*, although her mother still preferred to go out shopping in a *sifsaree*. Upon my return to Tunis in 1993, however, I was surprised to find that Shedia had stopped wearing the formal veil.

When I asked why, Latifa explained that the government's new poli-cies had forced Shedia to abandon the *hijab* or lose her job. It seemed that the new Ben Ali government had made a policy that forbade hiring veiled women for government jobs, their position being that women who had adopted the *hijab* would of course have adopted other conser-vative Islamic beliefs including the place of women at home—and therefore they would rather not be working anyway!

A third way in which young unmarried girls in Tunis move about outdoors is in large single- or mixed-sex groups, going to the markets, the cinema, or the zoo with friends of their own age. Janan, a twenty-year-old, unmarried high school student, explained in Arabic, "We go to Tunis, to the zoo, to the museum, to the beach a lot. A lot. To the market (*souk*) with Tunisian friends, in a group. Well, the markets, why not? It's not something wrong. We don't go out until one A.M. or midnight, you understand. We go out until about now [five P.M.]—girls with boys. We go out a lot. It's not a problem."

Socializing in groups allows the two sexes to interact without the danger of sexual relationships. For example, on the lawn of the Faculté de Lettres and at the Club Tahar Haddad, groups of male and female students can be seen standing or sitting together, laughing, talking, or working together on class assignments. Sidi Bou Said, a beautiful hilltop town near Tunis, is another favorite place for mixed groups of young men and women to stroll along the quays or drink tea in the outdoor hilltop cafés. (Sidi Bou Said is an unusual town, because women generally do not frequent cafés.)

However, although such group interaction is accepted by some of the more liberal middle-class parents and higher-educated young men and women, dating or private male-female relationships, in which sexual interactions may take place, are generally disapproved of except by the most liberal families. Indeed, the difference between the casual group friendships and more intimate male-female relationships is so significant that Tunisians have separate words for them, as Janan explained to me: "You say 'Sahibtee' for a female [friend]. For a man you don't say 'Sahibtee', you say 'Zameelee', someone who studies with me or works with me. You don't say 'Sahibtee' or 'Sahibee'. It's like we say it if, for example, he sleeps with her or goes with her to the cinema, or she stays out after midnight. That's why. It's the sense of it. It's not good."

Yet interestingly enough, perhaps the main restriction on unmarried women's interactions with men is not their parents but the opinion of other men. As Hannan pointed out in English, "Now girls are getting free. So most of the men, they look for a girl who either didn't finish her studies so she wouldn't expect him—she wouldn't ask for her rights like a university girl. She wouldn't ask such things. So they want only a woman who would be at home. You know, cook, wash, and stay there. Be a good wife for him and mother for their children. That's for, not for everybody. It's just now because the girls are getting really free and they want to do everything they want."

Hannan's words touch directly on a central paradox for Tunisian women: the increasing education of women, their entry into the workforce, and the apparent mixing of male and female activities prior to marriage, versus the continued expectation of virginity and the notion that after marriage, women will remain at home and focus on the domestic domain.

In my interviews and surveys a number of women described the restrictions on their freedom after marriage. Aya, a thirty-two-year-old high school–educated mother of two, who had donned the *hijab* in deference to the wishes of her husband, a university-educated engineer, lamented in French: "When I was little I lived in Megrine. We had neighbors, they were Italians. Sometimes they would have parties, receptions with their friends: there were Japanese, Indonesians, Italians, English, French people there. I was alone with my parents. My sister was married. They said to me, 'Come with us. You are alone. Come with us.' Those days were very wonderful."

"And now they are not?" I ask curiously.

"All that remains are my photos, because my husband forbade it," she answers forlornly.

Although young unmarried women are entering the workforce in increasing numbers, social pressures for married women to remain at home are reflected in the low percentage of women who work or continue their schooling after marriage. Indeed, even men who have been educated in Europe or the United States may prefer a wife at home, as in the case of Soraya, a forty-year-old *Tunisoise* woman whose husband had studied at a top university in Paris prior to their marriage.

"I wanted to work because as soon as I got married I took an exam to become a teacher," Soraya began in excellent French. "I succeeded in the exam and I taught for three months. And then my husband broke it off. He wanted to keep me at home."

Soraya's daughter, a high school student at the *lycée*, added, "He lived almost half his life in France. By living in Paris he was exposed to another mentality, another impression, another view. Yet when he returned to Tunisia, he still wanted to marry a Tunisian who would stay at home, who would have children."

Employment of women outside of the home after marriage—particularly in low-status jobs such as maids, factory laborers or hotel workers—is considered shameful, a sign that the husband cannot provide adequately for his wife and family or afford to seclude his women. As the affluent Belhedi family explained to me in a group discussion about class and work in Tunisia, one afternoon in the informal sitting room, "In the low-status jobs, if the woman continues after marriage it means she needs the money: resulting in shame for the husband." Women's work and seclusion are generally inversely related to class; only the poorest men who cannot afford to support their families alone send their wives out to work. Only two of the women whom I interviewed or surveyed, Miriam and Hind, worked in low-status jobs (both were maids) after their marriages.

Although it is becoming increasingly more difficult, working- and middle-class men in Tunis are still able to strive to maintain the family honor by keeping their wives at home. If finances become tight, women try to take on work in the home such as sewing, knitting, hairdressing, baking, or other domestic and handicrafts. Seven of the thirty-six women in my survey had home businesses: four women sewed clothes on commission for kin, neighbors, and friends; two women made and sold handknitted articles; and one woman operated a hairdressing salon for her clients out of her home.

Should finances turn, women's home businesses have the added potential of expanding into a true second income, as in the case of Latifa. Latifa had studied sewing during high school. After her marriage she continued to take in occasional projects, primarily wedding outfits for relatives and friends of the family. During my first field trip (1986–1987) Latifa made a small income, which she kept for pocket money to make personal purchases.

Upon my return in 1993, her husband Kareem's *auto-école* (driving school) had failed and he had gone into another venture, opening a small *tabac* (a mixed store of books, music, and curiosities). At the same time, Latifa's sewing business had started to boom and she had decided to rent a small store on a fairly well-traveled street where she could do her work and attract more customers. Latifa's venture into a business outside of the home unfortunately caused great stress on the marriage and, as a result, Kareem and Latifa were barely on speaking terms.

In the upper middle classes, the desire to maintain the family honor by keeping the wife at home may give way to the increased status and income that derives from women's work in prestigious positions in the government or teaching. Of the eight married women in my survey who were currently employed outside of the home, all but one (a maid) held prestigious positions in teaching or clerical/administrative work. These women enjoyed a significantly higher standard of living, in general, than the other women in the survey.

As these various cases illustrate, women in Tunis find many creative ways to adhere to the expectation that they remain at home while maintaining active economic and social lives. In describing their social activities, married women in my interviews would typically respond that they always were at home, *"deema fiddaree."*

For example, Nura, an uneducated migrant woman, whose network is described in Chapter 6, asserted quite definitely in Tunisian Arabic, when I asked her what social activities she participated in, "Every day I must stay at home alone. My husband doesn't like me to go out every day, every day. He wants the woman to be concealed." Likewise, Latifa, the woman who has her own sewing business, insisted in Arabic, "No, no I never go to weddings or parties. I am always at home."

These statements, however, were clearly an expression of the woman's virtue and honor more than a concrete reality, since in actual practice women often did not remain in their homes secluded from others. Latifa, for example, often had to help Kareem out at his driving school, taking calls and dealing with clients for his business whenever he had to be away. Likewise, Nura had a very active social life, not only visiting her parents and brothers and sisters regularly but also spending much of her day socializing in her neighbors' homes.

Being "in the home" in Tunis means different things to different women depending on their social class and economic and housing circumstances. For a poor migrant woman in the *medina* it may mean chatting in the courtyard to unrelated neighbors while cooking dinner; for a middle-class woman in the *lotissements*, visiting with friends in the park at the bottom of the high-rise building; and for an upper-middle-

A basket weaver's stall in the souks.

class woman in the suburbs, holding an evening party on the garden patio behind the house.

CLASS AND DOMESTIC SPACE IN TUNIS

The Medina

In Tunis, the *medina*, which literally means "city," refers to the original ancient Arab walled city that once received sailing ships from all over the Mediterranean. Today, the *medina* is the center of the Arab markets, or *souks*, where merchants and artisans cry out from their open stalls to passersby to buy their cloth, spices, clothing, housewares, and handmade crafts. As the crowd jostles along through the narrow, cobbled alleyways, women dressed in designer jeans and fashionable French clothing walk side by side with others wrapped from head to toe in *sifsarees*.

A quick turn off the main thoroughfares of the *medina* brings one suddenly into the quiet residential side alleys of ancient white-walled Arab houses. Composed of small sleeping and living rooms formed in a square around an open courtyard, Arab houses have no windows onto the street, ensuring the privacy of household activities.

Originally these houses were designed for large extended families, each nuclear family living in one of the rooms and sharing cooking, cleaning, and social activities (such as weddings and holiday celebrations) in the center courtyard. Today, however, the rooms are often rented by unrelated migrant men and/or their families.

In these Arab houses each household resides in one or two rooms, generally setting aside a corner of the room for cooking (commonly over a gas burner similar to American camping stoves). Since these Arab houses are quite ancient (some several hundred years old), many have limited and quite dated sanitation and electrical facilities. Most residents share a bathroom (with or without a flush toilet or bath), using the courtyard for washing dishes and clothes and for performing other daily domestic tasks.

Although household tasks such as cooking or the wash are not typically shared among unrelated neighbors, women living in these Arab houses often become friends with their neighbors living around the courtyard and will exchange favors such as baby-sitting or shopping for one another or will loan each other money or food in times of need.

Once the home of aristocratic *Tunisoise* families, the *medina* today houses a heterogeneous population of both older well-to-do original *Tunisoise* families and poorer migrants to the city.

The Villeneuve

The arrival of the French in 1881 saw the addition of a new French colonial city, the *villeneuve,* to the north and east of the *medina.* Tunis's *villeneuve* can roughly be divided into two primary areas: the business and apartment dwellings in the center and the wealthier French villas or garden residential areas to the north near the Belvedere park.

Square and flat-roofed, with whitewashed cinder-block walls, the villas of the *villeneuve* are reminiscent of their counterparts in southern France. To ensure the privacy of the female residents, these villas are typically surrounded by high cement walls enclosing a garden of orange and almond trees, jasmine bushes, and perhaps various herbs or vegetables. On warm summer evenings the garden is a favorite place for a stroll with guests or for a party on the outdoor patio.

Inside the one-, or perhaps two-, story villa, the formal salon (*beet sala*), furnished with European-style sofas and armchairs, is used on special occasions and to entertain outsiders. Close relatives and friends, on the other hand, sit together in the informal sitting room (*beet luq'ad*), where they can sit more comfortably on Arabic benches and cushions.

Reflecting the greater wealth of their inhabitants, villas typically include a bathroom and kitchen, complete with modern amenities such as a toilet, bathtub, and perhaps even a refrigerator or stove.

The downtown area of the *villeneuve* forms the central business district of Tunis. Tree-lined streets laid out in classic boulevard fashion are filled with honking cars, irate shouting taxi drivers, and crowded buses overflowing with riders hanging out of the doors and windows. Businessmen and businesswomen dressed in suits hurry down Avenue Habib Bourguiba, perhaps stopping for coffee or pastry at a French/Arabic *patisserie* before returning to work in one of the numerous banks, travel agencies, luxury hotels, government bureaus, and embassies lining the street.

In the area around Avenue Bourguiba one finds many shops, movie theaters, cafés, restaurants, and Tunis's concert hall and major department stores. On weekdays fashionable Tunisian women stroll up and down the promenade in the center of Avenue Bourguiba, pausing to gaze in the various shop windows. In the evenings and on Sunday afternoons, the streets are filled with men spending their free time at a café or a movie. And during the nights of Ramadan (the month of fasting), entire families swarm the streets to buy pastries and shop for clothes for their children. Only tourists and wealthy Tunisians frequent the expensive restaurants and concert hall.

Residents of the central *villeneuve* generally live in crowded apartments in three- to five-story colonial French buildings painted in pastel colors and decorated with louvered windows opening onto iron-grilled balconies. These aging buildings offer the amenities of electricity and plumbing installed (and never replaced) at the turn of the century.

The Lotissements and Cités Populaires

In 1921 the population of greater Tunis was estimated at a little over 190,000 inhabitants, almost half of whom were foreigners. By the time of Tunisian independence (1956), the population of the area had almost tripled, to 561,000. Much of this increase was due to the in-migration of Tunisians from the hinterland in search of employment. Today the population of Tunis and its surrounding suburbs is esti-mated at over 3 million, almost one-half of the population of the entire country.

Whereas many of the poorer migrants settled in the *medina,* the older parts of the *villeneuve,* or in rudely built shacks (*gourbis*) in undesirable areas around the city, a more highly educated, upwardly mobile middle-class migrant population sought out housing in the suburbs and ex-panding areas on the edge of Tunis.

In response to the growing demand for housing in Tunis, the gov-ernment commissioned numerous low- and middle-income housing projects, which now ring the city. These high-rise complexes form communities unto themselves. Complete with stores, parks, medical services, schools, and even day care programs, these *cités* allow Tunisian housewives to carry out their tasks in relative "protection" from the rest of the city.

Although the eight- to twelve-story apartment buildings generally have all the modern amenities—hot water, electricity, private bath-rooms, and kitchens—they were generally constructed with cheap ma-terials. Today, ten to twenty years after their construction, they suffer from peeling paint, broken elevators, cracked walls and ceilings, and poor insulation from rain and cold.

The *lotissements,* as these areas are called, are also the centers for many municipal complexes such as the university, the airport, the hos-pital, and the Olympic sports complex and football stadium—a favorite haunt of Tunisian men on Sundays. Near the northern *lotissements* are two contemporary shopping centers with large supermarkets, as well as a variety of chic stores selling luxury items at exorbitant prices. These enclosed shopping centers provide a less-exposed arena for women to do their shopping and are a popular spot for browsing either with girl-friends or as a family on weekends.

The northern area, referred to as the *menzehs,* has also become the center for new construction of lovely, well-to-do Arab homes and villas.

The Suburbs

Only thirty years ago, Tunis was a separate and distinct city from its suburbs, as Soraya, a forty-year-old, well-to-do *Tunisoise* woman described in French: "They [the migrants] are 'arrivistes'. They came and settled themselves in Tunis after independence. Before, we didn't have them. One was very much at ease because there weren't a lot of people. There was only the center of Tunis, the *medina* and then the little French corner where the Europeans lived. That was at Avenue Habib Bourguiba, there. That's all."

"Otherwise we only had little villages, the suburbs: Salambo, Carthage, La Marsa. There was also Manouba, and Le Bardo, too. There was Bardo, Manouba, Tunis, Ariana. Then after one left there were the north suburbs, beginning with La Goulette up to La Marsa, and the south suburbs, Hammam Lif. But all these houses, there weren't any. There was nothing in between. Only land and large fields."

The rapid influx of migrants (the "*arrivistes*" as Soraya pejoratively refers to them) has resulted in the merging of the suburbs with the city over the past years so that the distinction between areas is now blurred. Signoles et al. (1980) argue that, for Tunis, the term *banlieu* (suburb) should best be thought of as "urban fringe" or "urban sprawl" rather than as a surrounding ring of separate cities.

Like Tunis, the suburbs have experienced great in-migration in the past decades and include a mix of older Arab houses, a large number of French villas, their own adjacent *gourbivilles,* and various *cités populaires* and *lotissements*. In general, although these suburbs have their own market centers—and for Ben Arous and Megrine in the south, large industrial zones nearby—they have become primarily residential areas for the middle- and working-class sectors of Tunis.

The coastal suburbs, stretching from La Marsa to Hammam Lif, have the distinction of owning all of greater Tunis's beaches. Here numerous sumptuous villas (particularly in Carthage and La Marsa) line the beautiful coast, housing Tunis's elite as well as many wealthy foreigners. Although many of my interviews and observations for this study were collected within indoor spaces of women's homes in Tunis, it was to the beautiful sandy beaches of the northern suburb of La Marsa, as well as the more polluted urban beaches of Gammarth, that I went to collect my surveys.

And it was within the noisy, hectic walls of women's "private" homes that I learned about the essential rules of exchange and reciprocity that form the backbone of women's networks.

Notes

1. For a discussion of the origins of this "imprisoned" Muslim woman imagery, see Mabro (1991) and Graham-Brown (1988).

3
Tea and Visits:
Weaving the Web of Exchange

The tall concrete apartment building on the northern outskirts of Tunis had perhaps once been painted a cheerful peach. Now faded from too many searingly hot summers and drab rainy winters, it had, like its neighbors, blended into a pinkish gray punctuated by darker spots where the paint had peeled off altogether. As I walked up the concrete steps to the entrance, I tried to smile at some boys who were playing a kicking game with a few stones, oblivious to the late-afternoon chilling drizzle that had set in sometime at the end of November, and which would continue for several more months of mud-filled streets and alleyways before giving way to the dust and dazzling sun of the summer.

Inside the apartment building I took the stairs to the fourth floor, not wanting to wait to see if the elevator was working this time. I rapped the metal knocker at Latifa's door and a plump rounded face, hair tied neatly in a bun and ears accented by the ever-pervasive Tunisian gold jewelry, peeked out.

"Aslama," rotund, joking, twenty-seven-year-old Latifa welcomed me, smiling and with punctuated kisses, right, left, right on my cheeks, she escorted me in with a flurry of chatter. She smiled curiously as I handed over a plate of brown cakes.

"Chocolata Americaneea. Brownies," I explained as she whisked the plate off to her small but well-scrubbed tiled kitchen, well equipped by Tunisian standards with a sink and refrigerator and warmed by the simmering pots on her gas stove.

"Aq'ad, aq'ad (Sit, sit)," Latifa motioned to the informal sitting area, furnished simply with a flat, painted wooden Tunisian bench covered with brightly patterned cushions and a mumbling television that was displaying a Tunisian soccer match for Latifa's father, who was slouched in an armchair directly in front of it. Not interested in the game myself, I plopped down on the floor to play peek-a-boo with Mona, Latifa's dark-wide-eyed, one-year-old daughter, and Mounia, her thin, tall, four-year-old sister, as Latifa scurried back to the simmering smells in the kitchen.

A low, round wooden table soon appeared from the kitchen, clutched in the short, stocky arms of Kareem, Latifa's thirty-six-year-old husband, followed by steaming bowls of a spicy chicken-broccoli stew. Groaning inwardly I sat down to my second dinner that day; I had made the unfortunate mistake of a formal visit to the Belhedi family earlier that morning, where I had already eaten a sumptuous lunch of brik (a Tunisian fried egg pastry), couscous with octopus, a spicy fish in hot sauce, pickled turnips and carrots, and tangerines.

Politely I dipped pieces of my French baguette into the chicken stew, trying to wash it down with sticky-sweet glasses of Boga, a Tunisian soda, as the soccer game continued in the background.

"Zeed, zeed (Have more)," Latifa insisted, as all good Tunisian hostesses should. And so dutifully I slowly and painfully swallowed a few more bites.

Finally the meal ended. The television was turned around to face the formal sitting room, where Kareem, Bou Latifa, and I spread out on the contemporary upholstered brown corduroy couch and matching armchairs, nibbling on a plate of butter-and-almond-filled dates and sipping steaming glasses of peanuts floating in green tea that Latifa had set on the glass-topped table before us.

Several taps at the front door suddenly announced another Sunday visitor. Spilling vivaciously through the door with a heavy milk crate filled with oranges and a large box containing an iced layer cake from a Tunisian patisserie, Sarah, Latifa's bint 'amm (paternal cousin), and her husband excitedly kissed Latifa and her father hello, before greeting her new American friend.

Another round of glasses filled with tea and peanuts was now carried out on a brass inlaid silver tray for the new guests, along with a plate of juicy peeled mandarin oranges and Sarah's cake. Then, finally finished in the kitchen, Latifa sat down cross-legged on the floor next to Sarah and began animatedly exchanging news about their families and friends: the condition of Sarah's ailing father, Mounia's latest songs learned at the crèche (preschool), and who had commissioned the purple ruffled party dress that Latifa was currently sewing—for Latifa ran her own sewing business from her home.

At 9:30 P.M. another knock at the door announced the arrival of yet one more visitor, Latifa's brother, Nour. Realizing that I had been visiting for almost five hours, I thanked Latifa for her hospitality, promised to visit again soon, and, escorted by Kareem, waddled, far too well fed, down the stairs to the dark, rainy winter street below.

A simple Sunday visit to my friend, Latifa: the kind of social event that takes place in Tunis, as in many other homes throughout North Africa and the Middle East, every weekend, every holiday, every social occasion. Tea and food are served; guests arrive and leave unannounced; and relatives and friends exchange chit chat about their families, finances, cooking, clothing, and weddings.

On the surface these social visits seem to be rather casual, unstructured affairs. Visits can take place at almost any time of day or night; people arrive and leave whenever they please; and, with the exception of the requisite drinking of tea or coffee and eating of inordinate amounts of food, no overtly specific tasks or goal-oriented activities are engaged in.

Yet for women in Tunis, visiting is far from an insignificant private leisure activity. On the contrary, visits are serious and costly work: creating and maintaining the critical ties of exchange and support that define women's networks and the resources upon which they can count to survive in an increasingly impersonal and unpredictable urbanizing nation.

VISITS AND EXCHANGE

In Tunisia visits are characterized by the ritual exchange of food, gifts, and most important, the obligation to return visits given. During my visit to Latifa I gave her homemade brownies. Her cousin brought a very expensive cake[1] and a crate of fruit. Latifa, in return, plied her guests endlessly with special sweets, tea, and other delicacies. Latifa and her cousin also exchanged news and information about their families and Latifa's sewing business. And at the end of the visit, Latifa emphasized the importance of my visiting her again in the future.

Women use various terms to describe their visiting, and the implicit exchange and reciprocity that is the basis for network membership. Although women do use the verb "to visit"—*zeeara*—this term is generally reserved for long trips or for visits of respect, such as visits to an elderly person or at the time of a birth and during the wedding process. Thus, for example, women would say "*nzourhum fisseef*" (I go to visit them in the summer), when speaking of trips back to friends and family in their hometown each summer. Likewise, to indicate the respect given by the visit, especially to a very old person, women would also use the verb *zeeara,* as, for example, in the sentence, "*nzourou jidee fil'Eed*" (we visit my grandfather at religious holidays).

However, to describe more intimate, daily interactions, women generally spoke in terms of "seeing each other" or "coming and going."[2] Hence, to describe regular visits with friends or family, women would typically say: "*ana nshoufhe wa haya tshoufee*" (I see her and she sees me), "*nshoufou*" (we see each other), or "*ana nimshee wa haya tjee*" (I go and she comes).

Significant in their choice of words is the emphasis on physical contact (seeing each other or physically going and coming from each other's homes) and the implicit reciprocity and exchange expected in these visits (I see her and she sees me). A minority of educated and more well-to-do women in Tunis do maintain contact with kin and network members by telephone and letters, but these interactions are simply considered a supplement to the crucial face-to-face interaction required in all relationships. The most common way for a woman to indicate a break in social relations is to exclaim "*ana me nshoufhesh bikul!*" (I do

not see her at all). Of course, in the case of intimate kin—who by definition would have to come into contact occasionally—these exclamations
are an obvious exaggeration, intended more to emphasize the nature of
the relationship than actual physical experience.

Although the ideal relationship is truly reciprocal, women acknowl-
edge that due to various factors, such as distance, age, social position,
and transportation, some relationships are somewhat imbalanced, with
one member doing more of the "coming or going." Typically older
members of the family, and especially parents, receive more visits than
they give, as Soraya, the fourth in a family of ten children, explained:
"The one who visits most is always the youngest, who visits the older
ones. It is a respect for age."

Gifts, like visits, follow similar rules of reciprocation. An inadequately
returned gift will be quickly pointed out to shame the malingerer, as illustrated by an interesting little argument that occurred during my interview with Sherifa (see Chapter 5) when I asked what gifts she had
given recently.

"Sherifa gave me a bottle of perfume for my birthday," her *louza*
Kareema answered in Tunisian Arabic.

"It cost 25 dinars!" added Sherifa meaningfully.

"And at Sherifa's wedding I gave her 200 dinars," Kareema was quick
to put in. "What's 25 dinars for a bottle of perfume at a birthday, when I
gave her 200 dinars! It's nothing, 25 dinars."

This little debate is all the more intriguing since their claims of expensive gift giving were not only a debate about reciprocity but also
an effort to demonstrate to me, the American interviewer, their economic wealth. In personal terms these gifts were exorbitant, considering that the average monthly budget for each of these women was
only 200 dinars.

The importance of the rule of reciprocal exchange was emphasized to
me by Amal. A university professor and a divorcée in her late thirties,
Amal was trying to teach my husband and me about appropriate social
behavior in Tunisia: "These are the Tunisian customs. Always you give to
me and I give to you. What do you bring to me and what do I take to
you? You help me and I help you. If you don't come, then I will never go.
I'll never go!"

These explicit rules of exchange serve an important, unstated function: to delineate social, economic, and class boundaries.

CLASS, SOCIAL STATUS, AND VISITING NETWORKS

For women in Tunis, visits are an extraordinarily expensive and labor-intensive activity, as illustrated by Latifa's numerous offerings of dinner, tea with peanuts, stuffed dates, soda, mandarin oranges, and cake. Women are the hostesses, serving their guests endless rounds of tea and delicacies. They prepare the sweets and dishes and select the other gifts that are exchanged in visits. Finally, women are the main participants in visits, holding the primary responsibility for keeping in touch with both affinal and consanguineal kin. Women, then, do most of the *work* of visiting.

Considering that women in my survey visited an average of six households almost daily and another four households monthly, it is clear that visiting is a valued and essential part of women's daily lives. But why? Why would a working woman such as Hannan (see Chapter 7), who is heavily pregnant with her first child, choose to spend twenty or more hours per week visiting and hosting guests? Considering that after working all week she must then pluck the chicken for dinner (fast-food, microwaves, and TV dinners are simply not a part of daily life in Tunis) and devote her Saturdays to washing the clothes by hand and beating the living room rugs, it would seem more logical that she would spend her Sundays resting in peace at home. Likewise, why would Miriam (see Chapter 4), a poor maid with a newborn baby, a sister-in-law, and a sickly husband to feed on a meager income of 100 dinars[3] per month, prefer to spend her last remaining millimes on a bus ride to visit her in-laws every Sunday, instead of buying some meat or new clothes or medicine for her sick husband?

According to Hyde (1983), the importance of gift and social exchange in industrial societies lies not in the economic or political transfer of goods but in their symbolic meaning—creating and affirming bonds between giver and receiver. Gift giving thus becomes a ritual process in which the exchanges themselves serve as "tie signs": symbolic signs of the relationship between exchanging parties (Goffman 1971). Cheal (1988) expands this concept, suggesting that gift exchanges are used to define group membership and demarcate group boundaries, creating "small personal worlds" in the larger impersonal industrial economy.

Although Hyde's and Cheal's analyses emphasize the exchange of gifts or material goods, I argue that in Tunisia (and probably much of the Middle East) the exchange of *visits* serves a similar function: defining social and class boundaries and creating a "small personal world" of people upon whom women can depend in times of crisis or need. Hannan and Miriam do not spend their precious time and money on visits simply because they are fun (although visits are often enjoyable), but because visits are essential to their survival. In a face-to-face society, women's visits are a critical link to social and material resources, defining the status of the woman's household and providing the connections her family needs to jobs, services, information, and goods.

Because visits and hospitality must be reciprocal, their exchange is generally restricted to households of similar economic and social backgrounds. Visits thus reaffirm class, social, and regional boundaries.

Class, in Tunis, is a slippery concept, depending as much on the speaker and the speaker's aspirations and expectations as on any specific identifiable characteristics such as income. For women from original Tunis families (who refer to themselves as *Tunisoise*), class is defined in terms of one's region of origin and family history, Tunis families being, of course, the most prestigious category, followed by families from other ancient cities such as Sfax and Kairouan and the coastal Sahelian towns of Mahdia and Monastir.

Fatma, a married, educated *Tunisoise* woman who works for the government, emphasized the class distinctions between old urban families and rural migrants to Tunis: "People from the countryside, *baldi*, they are not liked in the society. They are not like educated people and they have all the problems. They don't know how to live and how to act. These are the people coming from outside Tunis. They are different from us. They don't think well. Even if you are kind to them they react differently."

A woman in a white sifsaree buys parsley in the central market of Tunis.

In contrast to *Tunisoise* women, in the eyes of wealthy, educated, upwardly mobile women from modest migrant origins, who are "shut out"
from the old aristocratic system, class is based primarily on one's wealth,
and to a lesser degree, one's position in the government and education.
This contrasting assertion of class lines was described to me by Jemila, a
nineteen-year-old migrant from a small town on the Sahelian coast who
was studying at the university. Jemila and I were discussing what factors
were important in choosing a husband, to which she replied, enthusias-
tically, in French, "Oh, that's a good subject!"

She continued, "In Tunisia there are two criteria: money and the family. Money and the name of the family—of the people. But to choose a
husband, well, nowadays it's beginning to be money is more important
than the name."

Hesitating for a moment, she elaborated, "In Tunis, the *Tunisoises*
speak a lot about the family name. The families that were originally
from here, have a reputation here. And it's very important for them because they *consider themselves*," she paused to repeat herself for empha-

sis, "but as I say, they *consider themselves* (*se prennent*)—because it's not true—as aristocrats. But as far as I'm concerned, one can't talk of an aristocracy in a country that doesn't have any royalty!" True to her criteria, a few years later Jemila married a wealthy factory owner from a rural area, the Cap Bon region.

The relationship of education to social status seems to be ambiguous at best. When I had completed my surveys, I asked two educated women to sort and categorize the women in the surveys by their *niveau social* (social class or level). One woman, Aida, a government employee and migrant to Tunis, began sorting the women first by the husband's profession, ignoring region of origin and education completely. When she realized I had also listed household income for each woman, she completely re-sorted the pile to reflect categories based solely on the monthly household budget.

Curious to understand her logic, I asked whether education was at all relevant, to which she replied, "No, what is education good for if you don't get money for it?" She went on to explain, "There are many cases of people here in Tunisia who don't have any education. But because they know the right people, they get high-paying jobs."

Zohra Belhedi, a school principal, was the second woman to sort the surveys; paralleling her daughter Jemila's criteria, the surveys were piled first according to income, with subpiles reflecting her assessment of the status of the husband's work within each economic category.

Although it would appear that these varying definitions of status-producing factors prevent any clear delineation of class boundaries in Tunis, I would argue that, on the contrary, class and social boundaries are quite distinctly drawn out, with clear rules about who belongs and how one can renegotiate and contest them. Social status claims and class boundaries are asserted and verified by the people with whom one can afford to exchange reciprocal visits.

Like the women in this study, I, too, created ties of support and assistance through my visits to various families. In contrast to the women in Tunis, however, to gain a representative cross-sample of women I deliberately participated in numerous distinct and unconnected networks and neighborhoods—of varying socioeconomic means—spread throughout the greater Tunis area.

WEAVING THE WEB OF EXCHANGE:
MEETING THE WOMEN IN THE STUDY

In one sense, my first field visit officially began on a blistering hot Sunday in September 1986. Arriving in Tunis, tired from an overnight journey by boat from Genoa, Italy, my husband, Lorenz, and I were overwhelmed by the spectacle of several hundred Tunisians streaming en masse toward the customs gate—pushing and shouting, nudging room for their overflowing colored woven sacks stuffed with gifts for their relatives and friends. We stumbled out the gate to be greeted warmly by Sami Belhedi, who would become, over the year, Lorenz's best friend; his family would become our adopted family.

But I must back up, for in reality my research on Tunisian visits and networks began unknowingly some six months earlier, with Mongi. Mongi was a Tunisian graduate student studying in the United States whom we met at an Arabic students' party at Northwestern University, where we were both studying. Hearing that my husband and I would be going to Tunisia in the coming year, he offered his assistance, and we offered our apartment as a sublet while we were gone. We invited Mongi to dinner at our place; he then reciprocated with a Ramadan dinner at his apartment.

And so, without knowing it, we became part of Mongi's network. Mongi introduced us to Sami Belhedi and Malik ben Cherifa, his Tunisian friends who were students at nearby universities. Malik had an uncle in Tunis, Monsieur Rjeb, whose apartment we ultimately rented. And Sami offered to show us around Tunis and get settled in, for he would be graduating and returning home to his family in Tunis that summer.

The Belhedis were one of the wealthiest families I would meet during my research,[4] with a monthly budget of 600 dinars; they owned three cars, a home in Manouba, and a rental home in the *menzehs,* and were in the process of constructing a vacation home on the coast. Both migrants from unskilled families in the central and Sahelian regions of Tunisia, Sami's father, Mohammed, was a successful *fonctionnaire* in the Tunisian government; his mother, Zohra, was a school principal. Unlike most couples of their generation, their marriage was a love match:

Mohammed and Zohra had met and secretly dated while they were both teachers at the same school.

Although Sami had found an excellent job as an engineer after returning from his studies in the United States, like many other unmarried adult Tunisian men and women, he chose to live with his parents in their house in Manouba, remaining there until his marriage six years later.[5] He shared a bedroom with his thirteen-year-old brother, Ibrahim. Likewise, his nineteen-year-old sister, Jemila, who was a student at the university during my first visit to Tunis, also remained in her parents' home until her marriage.

Moving In

Almost one month after our arrival in Tunis we moved into the newly constructed apartment of Monsieur Rjeb (Malik ben Cherifa's uncle or *khal*) in the rapidly growing area to the north of the city, called the *menzehs*. The apartment was in a two-story, white washed building that would ultimately have stores on the first floor. The second story had three apartments, all facing onto a common balcony. On our left-hand side lived Jasmina Binous, M. Rjeb's niece (his wife's sister's daughter) and her husband Ahmed. Both engineers, they had been married a little over a year and had no children. The apartment on our right remained under construction until the following summer, when it was rented to a single woman, a distant relative of M. Rjeb.

In contrast to our neighbors next door, below our apartments, in the rubble-filled future store area, lived Sharif, a migrant worker from the north of Tunisia who had been hired by M. Rjeb to complete the building. He lived without furniture, sleeping on a mat on the dirt floor and cooking on a small charcoal brazier. His situation, however, was a major improvement over the two migrant workers who lived across the street on the open balcony of the house they were building; at least he had a roof over his head and four walls. During the winter rains the two men had to endure sleeping huddled cold and wet under thin wool blankets as the rain pelted over the balcony, streaming in puddles around them. Sharif and the other migrant workers avoided us, somewhat bashfully nodding hello to their strange American neighbors. During bad weather and at Ramadan, Lorenz would go over with dishes of food or extra blankets, which were always returned neatly at our doorstep a few days later. Perhaps due to obvious class differences and/or because I was a foreign woman, I never, however, exchanged a single word with them.

Because the city had not kept pace with its growth, our apartment had running water and electricity (most of the time) but no telephone (only about 12 percent of all Tunis residents had phones at the time) or garbage pickup. As a result, many of the empty neighboring lots became enormous garbage dumps, filled eight to ten feet high with the inhabitants' debris.

When I came back to see our old home in the summer of 1993, the area had changed drastically, looking much more like a "neighborhood." The street had been paved; stores finally stood under our apartment; and most of the formerly garbage-filled lots were occupied by expensive new homes, complete with the now ubiquitous *paraboles* or television satellites that had taken over Tunis in the six years since my first fieldwork visit.

Friends and Networks

Over the first year of my fieldwork I became friends with a number of other unrelated women and their extended families living throughout the greater Tunis area. My friendship with the Belhedis led to my "affiliate membership" with their neighborhood street, and I came to know a number of the women and their families living on the street, including Douzha and her mother, Fauzia; Samia and her university student daughters, Lena and Lilia; Mounia, a widowed mother of three and her thirty-seven-year-old friend Neziha, who worked as a secretary; and Soraya, a forty-six-year-old *Tunisoise* woman.

My research affiliation with several academic organizations, plus my enrollment in Tunisian Arabic classes at the Bourguiba School (I had quickly discovered that Tunisian Arabic bore little resemblance to the standard Arabic I had studied in the United States), resulted in my friendships with Hannan, Faiza, Amal, and Najet. Hannan and Faiza were both married women who worked as bilingual secretaries. Hannan had an apartment in the rapidly expanding *lotissements,* while Faiza was living with her in-laws in an Arab house in the *medina.* Amal was a divorced, childless university professor in her thirties, who lived in an apartment in the *menzehs*. Najet was a university student in her mid-twenties, who resided with her parents and two brothers in a poor working-class neighborhood bordering the *medina*. Despite Najet's high educational level, both of her parents were illiterate. Her father owned a construction business where her brother was employed. Najet also had an older married sister, Ruaida, who lived next door and who frequently stopped by to visit.

It was through Kirstin, a Swedish exchange student at the Bourguiba School, that I met her host family, the Al Mohads, and their maid, Miriam, whose network is described in Chapter 5. And Hind, a forty-year-old maid, worked for one of the Americans whom I knew through the U.S. embassy. Both Hind and Miriam lived in the poor, undeveloped *populaire* quarters to the south of Tunis.

Finally, two extended families that I visited fairly often became friends by chance. I met Shedia, a high school teacher in her late twenties, and her mother while shopping on the Avenue Habib Bourgiba two months after my arrival in Tunis. Shedia had signed a marriage contract (*mlek*) and was therefore legally married to Ridha. However, since the formal wedding ceremony was not expected for another year or two (Ridha had not yet accumulated the necessary bridewealth), Shedia was still living with her parents and three brothers in the middle-class suburb of Le Bardo.

Shedia also had a married sister, Latifa, who lived about two kilometers away from her parents. I immediately liked Latifa, a cheerful, friendly, twenty-seven-year-old mother of two small children, and her husband, Kareem, who owned an *auto-école* (driving school), and we visited each other quite often. However, my friendship with Latifa caused quite an argument between the two sisters, for Shedia felt that since she had "discovered" me first, I should be *her* friend. Visits with Shedia, who wore the full veil or *hijab*, became even more strained in the spring when her husband, Ridha, was jailed for his participation in Islamist protests at the university. By the end of my first year of fieldwork in Tunis, we visited infrequently.

In February Lorenz met Tahar Ben Hamza, who was working as a tour guide at some archaeological ruins to the north of Tunis. One Saturday, a few weeks later, Tahar, who could not read or write and had no telephone (nor did we, for that matter), made the long two-hour trek on two different buses to show up at our doorstep and invite us personally to visit his family. We soon came to know his widowed mother, Umm Tahar; his uncle, Aberrahman; his married brother and wife, Sarah; and his two unmarried younger sisters, Siehen and Aymet, who all lived together in a simple, four-room, corrugated-roofed Arab house with no electricity or running water on the north edge of the Tunis sprawl.

Through my visits and exchanges with these women and their families, I came to learn the social rules for forming—and sometimes terminating—relationships in Tunis. As the following chapters illustrate, women's visits and exchanges—and the resulting networks—are intimately linked to the social and material resources each woman can offer to the relationship. Friendships and social ties are not simply a matter of luck and personal taste but the result of careful strategy and use of a woman's personal assets: her family name and reputation, her wealth, her education, her region of origin, or even her ability to cook.

Notes

1. Cakes and other sweets are extremely expensive for Tunisians. An average cake cost seven to ten dinars in 1987; almost a full day's wages. The high cost of this gift indicates the formality of this visit.
2. Abu Lughod (1986) observes a similar use of the verbs "coming and going" to describe visits among Egyptian Bedouin women.
3. The exchange rate was approximately $1.20 per dinar in 1987.
4. Although I occasionally attended U.S. embassy parties as part of my role as a Fulbrighter, I had little other opportunity to meet or socialize with the Tunisian upper class, whose lives and stories are not included in this study.
5. In Tunis adult children generally remain with their parents until their marriage for a variety of reasons: the shortage of housing in Tunis; the need to accumulate a bridewealth or dowry and otherwise save money for their anticipated marriage; expectations that adult children should contribute part of their earnings to their parents; and, especially for girls, social disapproval of people living by themselves without relatives.

4

Marriage and Family:
Miriam's Kin Exclusive Network

It is a hot, dry, quiet June afternoon. The women in the Al Mohad household are resting in the cool, dark sitting room of their elegant villa in the *menzehs*, languidly sipping green tea as we chat about my research. Miriam, their twenty-seven-year-old maid, is in the kitchen desperately hurrying to finish scrubbing down the sink, the tile counters, and the gas stove, the last of her chores for the day. Miriam usually catches the four o'clock bus, which brings her, an hour later, to her home—a simple concrete house without running water, a stove, or a phone—that she rents for forty dinars ($50) a month in a poor suburb south of Tunis. But today she is particularly pressed for time, because she has agreed to an interview with me before she leaves.

I had met the Al Mohad family through their Swedish foreign exchange student, Kirstin, who often sat next to Lorenz and me in our Tunisian Arabic class at the Bourguiba School. When Kirstin discovered that I was searching for Tunisian women to interview for my study, she suggested that Miriam might be interested, especially since I was willing to pay five dinars for her time.

Miriam was one of only two women, out of more than fifty-five survey and informal interviews, who ever actually accepted money for talking to me.[1] But then Miriam desperately needed it; her husband, Sami, worked sporadically as a laborer in construction projects, and his income was, as Miriam politely explained, rather "*th'aif*" (thin, weak). Which was why, despite the public shame and the fact that she had a three-month-old baby daughter at home, Miriam was scrubbing floors in someone else's house for about 50 dinars ($60) a month, ending up with a total household income varying between 100 and 135 dinars ($125–$175) per month.

My interview with Miriam begins very awkwardly. Afraid that "Madame," as she refers to her employer, will overhear what she is saying, we sit down in "Madame's" sewing room, a stuffy, windowless closet with a 1940s model sewing machine on a table piled high with plush, brightly colored cloth, gold-and-silver embossed lace, and other highly ornamental sewing notions. Sitting on a hard stool, thin, pale, in a simple cotton dress and twisting her hands nervously, Miriam begins, whispering so softly in Tunisian Arabic that I can barely hear her: "I was born in Tunis, but my family is from Hamma, in the south, near Gabes. I have two brothers and two sisters. They all live here in Tunis. My parents and my grandparents are dead. After my mother died I went to live with my older brother for three years, before I got married."

I ask Miriam if she visits her family very often, and if she ever goes back to Hamma, her family's hometown. She answers: "My older brother, I always go over there. The other brother, I don't see him a lot. I see my older sister sometimes, the other sister, no—at *'Eed* (holidays). I don't go to her often. Since I got married I haven't seen my *khal* who lives to the north of Tunis in Bizerte. My *'amm* (paternal uncle) lives far away in Gabes in the south near Hamma. I only have one *'amm*, that's all. He has children but I don't know them."

As Miriam explains, with the exception of her older brother, who lives in the same neighborhood, she only sees her younger brother and sisters occasionally because they live in other quarters of the city, requiring a bus ride to visit them. Likewise she only sees her uncles at special occasions, such as her wedding, primarily because it is too expensive to travel there—a round-trip to Bizerte by bus costs approximately four dinars or $5 per person and a trip to Gabes by *louage* (group taxi) runs approximately twenty dinars or $25 (one-half of her monthly wages).

Miriam and Sami have been married for one and one-half years and have just recently had a baby girl. Like Miriam, her thirty-two-year-old husband, Sami, was born in Tunis to migrant parents from the same hometown region. He, too, did not complete school past the sixth grade. Although the marriage was arranged and their income is limited, Miriam is happy with the choice, explaining, "He is a very good man. He does not drink and he prays."

We have been chatting for almost an hour when Miriam anxiously asks me what time it is. She cannot afford a watch, and I suspect she is not too comfortable reading one anyway, having left school before the sixth grade. Explaining that she must hurry to catch her bus, she promises to talk to me again next week.

One week later, Miriam is sitting before me again, in the same sewing room, in the same simple dress. But this time she is smiling and does not twist her hands nervously. She wants to listen to the cassette, to hear what I recorded in the last interview, and laughs, especially at my occasionally funny American-accented Arabic. And so we begin again, chatting about our families, our husbands.

"My husband is from my brother's wife's family in Medenine [a town in the south of Tunisia, near Miriam's hometown of Hamma]. It was my older brother who chose him—my mother and father were dead. I was here in Tunis, and my husband was here in Tunis.

"Because my brother's wife is family, we are very very close. . . . All of my husband's family know my older brother much better because his wife is from the family."

Being relatives already prior to their marriage, Miriam is also very close to her husband's family and visits them frequently. "My *hmou* (father-in-law) and *hmet* (mother-in-law) live about four kilometers away in Sejoumi with my two *louzet* (sisters-in-law). We always go there. Almost every Sunday we eat over there."

Miriam is not the only one in her family to marry a relative. Miriam's younger brother married his *bint khal* (maternal cousin) and her *khal* (maternal uncle) married his *bint 'amm* (paternal cousin).

Sami has a married sister who lives a little farther away in the town of Mornag, where Miriam's younger sister, Jasmina, also lives. But, as

Miriam explains, "His sister, no. I don't always go to her. She comes sometimes, but I don't go. At *'Eedet* (religious holidays)."

Perhaps most significantly, however, Sami's sister, Manil, currently lives with Sami and Miriam and takes care of the baby while Miriam is at work. Although Miriam is glad to have Manil's help, she still feels the situation is very difficult, as she explains when I ask her if she wants any more children. "I would like to have a girl and a boy. But I don't know. Not now. Maybe after a long time. Four years or so. Because I work. We don't have our own house or work for my husband. My husband is always sick."

Although Miriam sees Sami's family frequently, they do not visit his extended family because of the distance. "My husband's family: He has family in his hometown. But right from the beginning I never knew them. He has a grandmother and grandfather. I don't know them at all. They are in Medenine."

In addition to visiting the small circle of seven relatives and their households, Miriam has one very close girlfriend who lives next door to her. "With my friend I go to the *hammam* (Turkish baths). We hang out in the evening. She is a very close friend, but because she works and I work, I can't visit with her all that long. I have known her fifteen years. We went to school together. She got married first before me. I see my friend every day, especially on Sundays."

"And these are all the people that you visit?" I ask. "There's no one else, like a neighbor or . . ."

I am surprised. I know that Miriam is a maid, and that she sees Madame—her employer—and Madame's family almost every day. What about *le patron* (your employer), I prompt. Silence. Miriam looks down awkwardly and shakes her head silently, as if to say, "No, not Madame."

We move on to other subjects, questions about the people Miriam turns to for help, about Tunisian wedding and religious traditions, and about her expenses and household budget. It is clear from the interview that even though Miriam does not consider Madame part of her network—a choice that is underscored by her use of the formal French word "Madame" to address her Tunisian employer[2]—over the past three years that she has worked for the Al Mohad household her employer has played an important role in assisting Miriam, especially during important life cycle events. For her wedding, Madame contributed substantially to Miriam's *zhez* (dowry) of dishes, curtains, and towels. In addition to giving Miriam gifts for her wedding, Madame also gave her gifts of clothing for the baby when she was born. And over the years that Miriam has worked for her, Madame has loaned Miriam food and money when she has needed it.

The interview ends well, and I pay Miriam her five dinars. After I close up my notebooks and stow away the tape recorder, we continue to chat, this time informally, as we walk together to the bus. It is later, when I sit down to write up my notes and analyze the interview, that I finally realize why Miriam had paused so awkwardly in response to my question about Madame; for visiting networks are based on ties of reciprocity and exchange, not obligation and service as in Miriam's patron-client relationship with her employer. No matter how close a maid may become to the family she works for, they are not from the same social worlds, they do not visit one another's homes, and they can never expect to exchange gifts and services equally.

THE IMPORTANCE OF FAMILY: KIN EXCLUSIVE NETWORKS

Miriam's network typifies the most basic and central pattern of women's social ties in Tunis: a network centered around kin. Although Miriam does include one close long-term friend in her network, her social ties are almost exclusively with kin. Approximately one-third of the women in my survey had a network style similar to Miriam's, a pattern that I have labeled the "kin exclusive network." Like Miriam, the women in my study with kin exclusive networks restricted their interactions almost completely to kin, including at most one or two friends or neighbors in their social circle.

In contrast to Miriam's pattern, the other two network patterns described in this study—the "neighbor network" and the "friendship pattern"—include nonkin such as neighbors or friends. However, as Table A2.1 in Appendix 2 indicates, regardless of the inclusion or exclusion of friends and neighbors, all three network styles are composed of a large core of kin. In all three network patterns, kin typically form between two-thirds to all of a woman's network. Women reported visiting, on the average, twelve households of kin on a regular basis, in contrast to an average of only four households of nonkin. Statistically, there is no significant difference in the mean number of kin in women's networks according to network type. However, women with kin exclusive networks visited significantly fewer households than women with either of the other network types. This suggests that *friends and neighbors do not replace kin, but become supplemental social resources* added to the basic social pattern of a network dominated by, and strongly dependent on, kin.

The central importance of kin in Tunisian women's lives is illustrated not only by the high proportion of relatives in their networks but also by the continued practice of marriage with kin.

KEEPING THE FAMILY TOGETHER:
ENDOGAMY AND KIN NETWORKS

Miriam, like 54 percent of the women in my survey, married a relative, a man from her brother's wife's family. Her younger brother married his maternal cousin (*bint khal*), and her uncle (*khal*) married his paternal cousin (*bint 'amm*). Much has been written on the Arab practice of endogamy, and in particular the preference for marriage to one's parallel cousin, or *bint 'amm*. Arab intermarriage has been argued to reinforce kin ties, keep wealth within the family, and increase parental control and protection of daughters. Rates of endogamy seem to vary significantly over time and place in the Middle East, and Meriweather concludes after reviewing the evidence that "the supposed cultural evidence for lineage endogamy is not as straightforward as much of the literature would suggest" (1999, p.134). This may in part be due to varying definitions by researchers of closeness of kin.

In my study I simply asked women to define their relationship to their husband, which yielded a very high percentage of answers indicating marriage to a relative.[3] Interestingly, despite the supposed preference for marriage with patrilateral kin, and in particular, one's paternal cousin, in my survey only about half (47 percent) of the marriages to kin were with paternal cousins. The remaining endogamous marriages were to maternal cousins (21 percent), exchange marriages—for example, two brothers marrying two sisters (16 percent)—and unspecified kin (16 percent). Endogamous marriage, ultimately, collapses the kin network onto itself: One's uncle (*'amm*), for example, becomes also one's father-in-law in cousin marriages. Trying to untangle the actual kinship ties of women in my interviews often became a hilarious experience as women would patiently try to walk through the complex interrelationships between members of their network. Yet while, in one sense, endogamy strengthened and reinforced existing ties between kin in women's networks, intermarriage also had the reverse effect of shrinking the network and ultimately reducing the social resource base upon which kin could draw. Thus, curiously, women who married kin had significantly fewer relatives in their networks than women who married outsiders.

Interestingly, marriage to kin was not related to either the husband's educational level or household income. In contrast, women with more years of schooling were statistically more likely to marry outsiders, suggesting that education may be linked to women's greater autonomy from the family. (See Table A2.4 in Appendix 2.) Women's education and employment, however, do not necessarily imply their independence from kin, as Anissa's story illustrates.

Anissa, like Miriam, is a migrant woman who has a relatively small kin exclusive network of nine kin households, which she visits on a regular basis. Like Miriam, she is a working mother; she is thirty-five years old, with four children, and works for the government ministry. Unlike Miriam, however, she is quite educated by Tunisian standards, having studied at the *lycée* until the *bac* (high school completion exam). Her husband, Hamid, who works in administration at the University of Tunis, also studied up to the *bac*. Together, from their two paychecks they earn about 300 dinars a month.

Hamid is Anissa's *wuld 'amm* (paternal cousin and preferred spouse in Arab society). Although Anissa had a voice in accepting her spouse, she explains, "He was chosen for me." Hamid and Anissa were both born in Kairouan (about 120 kilometers, or a three-hour trip, from Tunis). Hamid moved to the capital twenty years earlier seeking employment opportunities but preferred to choose a bride from his hometown.

After their marriage, Anissa joined Hamid in Tunis, where they have lived in the same downtown apartment for the past fourteen years with Hamid's divorced mother. Anissa has two married brothers, who live near her in two separate apartments in the same building in Tunis. She also has three married sisters and a brother, who lives with and cares for her mother, in Kairouan. In contrast to Miriam, Anissa and Hamid earn enough money to make regular trips to their hometown. The two of them try to return to Kairouan to visit their joint relatives (her relatives are also his kin since they are cousins) at least "every three months." If possible, they also prefer to spend religious holidays and celebrations in their hometown. Most recently they elected to celebrate their son's circumcision in Kairouan during the religious holiday of *'Eed ekkabeer.*

The only other person in Anissa's network is her paternal uncle, *'amm,* who lives in Tunis. "[I see him] at special occasions. If he is sick, if he went on a trip or something I visit his family. If not, every *'Eed* (holiday) or celebration." When asked whether Anissa had any friends outside the family she replied, "No, absolutely not. Because I work. I don't have time. It's work, family, and the education of my children that's most important."[4]

Anissa provides an interesting contrast to Miriam. She is educated and well-to-do, and thus can afford to return to her hometown regularly. However, her network still remains small, perhaps in part because her in-laws are her own natal kin. She also married a man from her hometown, even though he was living and working in Tunis at the time, a pattern common to two-thirds of the women in the survey. Only 20 percent of the women married someone not known to the family, emphasizing the continuing importance of familial ties and parental opinion in selecting a mate.

VISITS AND MARRIAGE

Selecting a spouse in Tunisia can often be a difficult choice fraught with potential conflict. One of the main reasons for this is that in the Arab world marriages are not made between individuals but between families that are then inextricably bound in a social network of ties that may last for generations. Historically, as in Anissa's and Miriam's cases, marriages were arranged, giving the parents control over the alliances that would result. However, in contemporary Tunisia, although arranged marriages still persist (almost one-quarter of the women in my study had their spouses selected for them), women and men are increasingly having a say in selecting their own mate.

Mate selection, however, is not easy in a culture where it is inappropriate for women to interact with men outside of their immediate family, and where premarital sex is still considered forbidden.[5] Many couples meet each other, therefore, through family get-togethers and visits where relatives or friends of the opposite sex are present. For example, Aziza, a thirty-three-year-old *Tunisoise* woman, who had studied up through secondary school, met her husband, who was a friend of the family, during visits to her maternal uncle's house.

"How did you get to know your husband?" I ask.

Aziza answers, "I knew him. I went to the house of my *khal* in La Goulette—my uncle knew him."

"And he was at your uncle's house?"

"Yes," Aziza nods.

As Aziza's story illustrates, visits to relatives not only are a central part of maintaining family ties but also play an interesting secondary role of matchmaking, allowing men and women to meet and see potential future spouses. It is perhaps not surprising, then, that the majority (74 percent) of the women in my survey married either kin or friends of the family.

For those women who did not select spouses known to the family, the potential for friction is high, as Latifa's story illustrates. Latifa, a twenty-seven-year-old *Tunisoise* mother of two who had studied up through secondary school, had fallen in love with her migrant neighbor's brother Kareem, but faced such opposition to the match that she decided to elope with him. This move left her without any financial assistance for the marriage, as she explained to me when I was interviewing her in a mixture of Tunisian Arabic and French about typical articles in a Tunisian *mahr* (bridewealth) and dowry (*zhez*): "Well, my husband and I, that's another story. I didn't have a *zhez*. At all, at all. My husband

A young woman with hands stained with henna, a sign of happiness at weddings and other celebrations.

bought the bedroom furniture and a refrigerator and stove. That's all. . . . In the beginning we didn't even have a television!"

"And your family didn't give you anything?" I ask, surprised.

"They didn't give me a thing. Even my wedding clothes—it was Kareem who bought them. My family was truly against it."

Despite Latifa's family's opposition to the match, however, they did not cut visiting ties with her after her marriage. In fact, Latifa, who lived only a mile away from her parents, visited her mother several times a week. Upon my return to Tunis in 1993, Kareem had even gone into business with his in-laws, opening a *tabac*, a small store carrying cigarettes, music, and small favors, that he ran with the assistance of Latifa's brother and father.

Even so, the marriage was not a happy one. Latifa would make pejorative jokes about Kareem's "country cousins" in the Cap Bon, who were illiterate weavers. And on my last field visit Kareem was seriously considering working abroad to get away from the tension in the household without having to resort to divorce.

As in Latifa's case, women's educational level was significantly related to whether they would marry an outsider. Women with higher education, especially at the university level, typically have experienced more freedom from the household. Often their lengthened years of schooling allow them to meet men outside the home when they are of marriage-able age. And many of the more educated women hold jobs in mixed-sex offices, where they can meet potential spouses.

At the university, interaction between young men and women is fre-quent enough that dating and premarital sexual relations do occur, not always in the best interest of the woman, as the case of Najet, a twenty-six-year-old student at the University of Tunis, illustrates. Najet came from a modest and fairly illiterate migrant family; her mother had no schooling and her father, who had not studied much more, owned his own construction business. Neither Najet's older sister nor her brother had studied past high school, but somehow Najet had done extremely well in her studies and continued on to university. When she was in high school, her family had arranged her marriage to a cousin from their hometown in Cap Bon. But Najet had vehemently refused, and the en-gagement had been broken off.

Several years later Najet met Muhammed, another student at the uni-versity. They had fallen in love, and Muhammed had proposed marriage to Najet's family. Her parents, however, had refused since he was a Berber. But the relationship had continued in secret, and for the past two years they had been having sexual relations. This had placed Najet in an extremely compromising position, which was causing her great distress when I met her. At twenty-six, no longer a virgin, and highly ed-ucated, she would have difficulty marrying someone else. And yet mar-riage to Muhammed seemed out of the question.

Najet's romance, which follows the contemporary Euro-American pattern of dating and sexual relations before marriage, is far from typi-cal in Tunisia, however. Whereas in the United States couples generally meet, date, fall in love, and get married, in Tunisia it is the reverse: Couples meet, they marry, then they date, and, hopefully, fall in love.

The Marriage Proposal and Bridewealth

Although often today the prospective bride and groom may have seen and talked to each other at social occasions, the decision to marry continues to lie with the parents, who may or may not consult with their son or daughter about their wishes. The marriage process thus begins officially with a visit by the prospective husband's family to the future bride's family. During this visit, called the *youm elkhutouba* (day of engagement or betrothal), all of the major expenses of the marriage are negotiated: the bridewealth,[6] trousseau (*zhez*), and number of celebrations to be held.

Latifa describes the proper way to contract a marriage (in contrast to her own disastrous efforts): "In my sister Shedia's case, the day when her husband asked for her hand in marriage, they decided everything. They said, for example, who will prepare the furniture, the TV, the refrigerator or stove, the curtains, the sheets, the bedspreads, the dishes. Everything, everything, everything. Even the mattresses and her clothes too."

The number of gifts and the expense of the celebrations will, of course, vary considerably depending on the wealth of the extended kin groups. An elaborate bridewealth may cost tens of thousands of dinars, or several years' wages for a man with a good job. Not surprisingly, negotiations over the costs and nature of the bridewealth and wedding celebrations can often be quite serious and sometimes contentious. And crises such as the loss of a job for the husband may delay or even terminate the engagement, as in Shedia's case.

Just prior to my first field visit, Latifa's twenty-eight-year-old sister Shedia had signed a *sdeq* or legal marriage contract with Ridha, a young man she had met at the University of Tunis. In contrast to Latifa's disastrous choice, her parents were happy with the match: He was highly educated, had a good job as a teacher of religion at a private school (as did Shedia), and came from an acceptable family.

However, the engagement soon began to turn sour. First, Ridha's mother insisted on selecting the engagement ring, an emerald that both Shedia and her mother felt was of poor quality. In response to their complaints, Ridha's mother objected to the white satin pillows that Shedia had provided for the engagement party, and unfortunately spilled some *henna* on one of them during the *henna* celebration. These, however, were minor quibbles, and Ridha continued to visit Shedia's house and occasionally take her for a stroll along the seaside boulevard at Sidi Bou Said on nice Sundays.

Unfortunately, toward the end of my first year of fieldwork Ridha became actively involved with one of the religious opposition groups and was arrested and jailed during one of the group's protest demonstrations. His imprisonment ultimately cost him his job and his wife. Upon my return to Tunis in 1993, Shedia's family had broken off the marriage.

Not all families require elaborate and expensive wedding gifts and celebrations. Marriages with kin are frequently not as expensive, because both families know and trust one another, as Nahla, a twenty-five-year-old Sahelian woman who moved to Tunis to marry her *wuld 'amma* (paternal cousin), explains, "Some people pay a lot of *mahr* (bridewealth). It depends for each person. Because my husband was from the family, he didn't pay a large *mahr.*"

Poor families, also, may dispense with elaborate preparations that they cannot afford, as in Aziza's case. Aziza was a thirty-three-year-old *Tunisoise* woman who had met her husband through visits with her *khal*. She had studied sewing in secondary school, and prior to the birth of her first child three years before had worked in a sewing factory. Her husband, a migrant from the south of Tunis, was a waiter with only a few years of schooling, and at the time of my interview their household had one of the lowest incomes in my study, eighty five dinars a month. They got married when Aziza was twenty-seven, a late age for women in Tunis. Her parents had died a few years prior to her marriage, and she had remained at home with her seven unmarried brothers—most of whom were unemployed—and two unmarried sisters, supporting herself and them by working at the factory.

"We didn't do anything because we didn't want to," Aziza explains in Tunisian Arabic. "We said, 'Don't bother. Just have the wedding.' Because I am old, I'm the oldest of my sisters, and they're not married. So we didn't do anything. We just went to the municipality, wrote the *sdeq* (marriage contract), and left."

"You didn't have a *hafla* (party) at all?" I ask, surprised.

"Nothing at all. By God, only the wedding ring. . . ."

"He couldn't afford it, and I was working. He couldn't afford anything: only the bedroom. That was it, that was all he bought me."

A man dances to a traditional band at a wedding. The scarf on his hips is used to accentuate his hip movements.

Engagement and Legal Marriage

Once the basic costs of the marriage have been settled on, one or two formal engagement parties may be held: a *fetiha* (where the opening *soura* of the Quran is read) and/or a *mlek* (a celebration of the signing of the marriage contract). The number of engagement celebrations depends, in part, on when the wedding contract (*sdeq*) is signed. Some couples will wait until the week of the social wedding to sign the contract. In other cases, as for example with Shedia, the parents of the girl may be concerned that the fiancé will change his mind, or that a long engagement period may lead to questions about the girl's virginity. In these situations, the contract may be signed immediately upon engagement or at a later date between the *fetiha* and the actual wedding.

After the contract is signed, the couple are legally (although not socially) married and must file for a divorce if the arrangement is not satisfactory. Hence, in Shedia's case, although she had never lived with Ridha or consummated the marriage, she had to get a divorce. By the time she filed for the divorce she was thirty. Upon my return to Tunis, it seemed unlikely that at age thirty-four she would ever remarry.

According to the older Tunisian women I interviewed, in the past engagements were reportedly rather brief, lasting a few months to a year, as Naima, a fifty-year-old migrant woman who had married her aunt's husband's son, explains in Tunisian Arabic: "I didn't wait to get married like these days—three or four years, no. As I said, years ago once you had the *mlek* you had to get married after six months, four months." One of the major reasons for such long engagements today is that women in Tunis often prefer not to live directly with their in-laws, necessitating the preparation of an entire house or apartment, rather than simply a room in the husband's parents' home, as in the past. Naima continues, "In the past the husband brought a watch, clothing, a little, very little. A little clothing, a few dishes. But now, it's a lot."

"Now you need the whole kitchen," her daughter adds. "The rugs, the stove."

Advertising, foreign films and magazines, and tourism have also contributed to the increasing demands of future brides, who now have fantasies of a husband who can offer them a house with a television, a refrigerator and stove, a washing machine, and a car. Unfortunately many of these items are financially out of the reach of all but a select well-to-do elite, causing great dissatisfaction and disillusionment for some.

In 1993, upon my return to Tunisia, import restrictions had been lifted significantly and stores began to carry many foreign items previously unavailable unless one could afford a trip overseas. Instead of making most Tunisians happy, however, the presence in shop windows of unaffordable luxury items such as forty-dinar toasters and two-hundred-dinar coffeemakers only appeared to increase people's frustration. As Latifa commented to me, "I dream, I dream, but it's impossible to attain what I want." She then added disconsolately that she had learned that "although of course one should have dreams, they shouldn't be too great or you might face immense disappointment."

Given the economic realities of high unemployment and underemployment and rising housing prices, many couples are discovering that they have to wait years to afford the escalating dowries and bridewealth that they have signed for in the contract.[7] Many of the women I interviewed worked prior to their marriage primarily to pay for their dowry.

Mousim Visits

The lengthy *fitra elkhutouba* (engagement period) is not only a period to allow for the accumulation of the bridewealth and trousseau, however, but also a time for the two extended families to establish social bonds of exchange and obligation, and for the couple to get to know each other. Whereas in the past women would often see their husbands for the first time on their wedding night, most contemporary Tunisian men and women, even with arranged marriages, expect to meet and become acquainted with their future spouses prior to the actual wedding. Sometimes, in more liberal families, the future couple is allowed to "go out" or meet in public places together, perhaps taking a stroll along one of the seaside boulevards, as Shedia did, or going to family social events together such as the Ramadan dinner at Hannan's apartment (described in Chapter 7).

More typically, however, among conservative families, the couple meets and socializes during formal visits by the prospective husband to his bride's house during major and minor religious occasions, called *mousim*. During these holidays, the future husband and his family are expected to visit the bride's family, bringing food and gifts. Commonly, the girl then includes these gifts with her trousseau.

In return the girl's family usually prepares an elaborate meal for her prospective in-laws, as was done on a *mousim* visit that Lorenz and I made along with Tahar ben Hamza and his family, at 'Eed ekkabeer (the holiday of the sacrifice of a sheep).

Tahar had met his bride, Behija, through his younger sister Zakia, who worked with Behija in a nearby sewing factory. On the second day of the 'Eed, Lorenz and I accompanied Tahar and his family to his future bride's home in the countryside a few miles from his home on the northern outskirts of Tunis.

We arrived at Tahar's fiancée's house: They were poor-looking farmers with a number of sheep and a few other animals. The house was based on a large courtyard with two rooms on one side: One was the kitchen in which the slaughtered 'Eed sheep was hung, and the other was the bedroom/living room to which we were led. In this room we found Umm Tahar (Tahar's mother), Tahar's unmarried sister Siehen, Tahar's older brother, Abdul, and his wife, Sarah, plus Sarah's father (Tahar's father was dead). Behija's (his fiancée's) mother and father were there, but his fiancée was not.

The men sat around one table to the right, and the women around a second table to the left. Almost immediately after arriving we were served a large meal consisting of couscous with lamb, a lamb stew, tajine (a baked egg dish), another lamb stew, bread, and watermelon. All of the dishes were served in a communal bowl for each dish, into which everyone dipped their bread and ate. We were also served soda and water, again in communal cups. After the meal we were served thick heavy tea with almonds.

Tahar's family had brought three baskets of gifts for Behija and her family. The baskets contained the following items:

> *One wicker basket containing food: bread, soda, meat (which had already been taken by Behija's family and put to use in the dishes, according to Umm Tahar), tea, spaghetti, canned tomato sauce, canned harissa (a hot spicy sauce), a box of biscuits, and sweet jellies;*
>
> *One wicker basket containing traditional beauty items (henna, teeth-cleaning bark, natural chewing gum) and a water service (jug and glasses);*
>
> *One satin-lined basket (which belonged to Tahar's sister-in-law, Sarah, who had received it for her wedding) containing gifts for Behija, Tahar's fiancée: shampoo, perfume, and a jaleba (traditional Tunisian robe).*

By the end of the engagement period, the husband's family has offered numerous gifts to his bride and her family through the many *mousim* visits and engagement celebrations. The bride's family, in return, has been the host to its future in-laws, serving elaborate meals and sweets at the frequent visits and celebrations. When the wedding week finally arrives, both kin groups have already established many reciprocal network ties of exchange and obligation.

Visits and Parties During the Wedding Week

During the week before the wedding night, the bride and groom each undergo various purification rituals such as bathing at the *hammam* (Turkish steam baths), removing all bodily hair (*tunqeea*), and staining parts of the body (particularly the hands and feet) red with *henna*. Often these rituals are celebrated by small parties in the home of the bride or groom, where friends and relatives of the same sex come to visit and eat cakes and tea.

The small get-togethers of the wedding week finally culminate with the actual wedding celebrations. These parties are large, expensive affairs to which hundreds of guests may be invited. In the past, and still in some of the more popular quarters and in the countryside, these wedding celebrations are an open community or neighborhood affair, held in the courtyard or garden of the family. Yet in more recent years more well-to-do families have begun to hold more "private" events in large rented halls, where guests may attend only by invitation.

The costs of these numerous celebrations can be quite exorbitant, as Amal, a divorced professor at the University of Tunis, points out in Arabic, "Do you know how much money someone needs for a wedding? They need a thousand or a thousand five hundred or five hundred dinars." Given that at the time of my research, the typical household earned an average of 2,665 dinars a year (Institut National de la Statistique 1999), one celebration alone would therefore cost a family approximately five months' wages.

The numerous celebrations, gifts, and ritual visits of the marriage process both create and perpetuate existing social ties in several ways. First, the many *mousim* visits and gifts from the husband's family to his bride's family establish bonds of obligation and reciprocity between future in-laws. Second, both sides of the family invest immense amounts of money in the future couple through the practice of providing a bridewealth, a dowry, and numerous wedding celebrations. And finally, the preference for endogamous marriage strengthens already existing ties with the kin group.

Notes

1. Hind, also a maid, was the only other woman to accept payment for my interviews.
2. Language use is a significant social indicator in Tunisia, revealing preferences about one's aspired status, education, ideologies, and contact with outsiders and foreigners. For an Arabic-speaking maid to address her native Arabic-speaking employer as "Madame" reveals many levels of meaning. It can be seen as a sign of respect and formality: the notion that "Madame" is part of the upper-class French-educated elite. It can also be seen as a way of distancing: the concept that "Madame" is not really Arab or Tunisian but essentially a foreigner.
3. The rates of kin endogamy reported by women in this survey fall between previously very high figures of up to 75 percent in one rural community (Cuisenier 1960) and significantly lower postindependence rates of between 13 and 19 percent (Bouraoui 1986). Bouraoui, however, bases his figures on marriage records, which have a much more restrictive definition of consanguineal marriage than this study. In the survey, women were permitted to identify their relation to their husband even if quite distant. Notably, Bouraoui finds no evidence for a decrease in rates of intermarriage over the period he studied (1970–1982); indeed, he argues that rates of endogamy have remained surprisingly stable.
4. One could theorize that Anissa's and Miriam's small networks are perhaps due to their employment. However, women's employment in general appears to be positively (not negatively) related to network size for my sample.
5. Naamane-Guessous' (1988) revolutionary survey of Moroccan women's sexual activities radically brings into question the degree to which most young women in North Africa today observe norms of virginity.
6. Technically, the legal limit of the brideprice (naqd or mahr) has been set at one dinar in Tunisia. As a result, large payments of money are often no longer given to the bride and her kin. (There are, of course, still numerous cases where the law has been ignored and larger sums of money paid.) Instead, the husband is expected to furnish the couple's future home and bring gifts of gold, perfume, etc., to his prospective bride.
7. This enormous escalation of the bridewealth is also occurring in Egypt, as described by Singerman (1995) and Hoodfar (1997).

5
Sherifa's Street:
Migration, Residence Patterns,
and Kin Networks

It is a blistering hot July afternoon, and I am dressed for another day at the beach, carrying a bag filled with suntan lotion, a tape recorder, spare batteries and tapes, five copies of my survey, a glass bottle of water, and a *kaskrout* (Tunisian fried egg and hot sauce sandwich). Lorenz has just dropped me off at the Le Marsa beach, and I wave good-bye to him as he drives off on our moped to his Arabic class.

I sit down inconspicuously at the back of the beach on a slight bluff to get my bearings and to gather my courage. This is always the most difficult moment of my survey research: talking myself into walking up to a group of women under an umbrella and saying, *"Aslama, n'amal bahath 'an elniss'a wa el'aila ettuniseea"* (Hi, I am doing a study on Tunisian women and the family.).

I will only be turned away by two women—women alone, without other relatives and friends around them—out of thirty-eight interview requests. And yet, still, before each interview I will have a lurching feeling in my stomach, my mouth will feel dry, and for a moment I will regret that I have asked Lorenz to come back on his moped to pick me up several hours later at five in the evening.

And so I sit on the beach delaying for a few minutes, checking and rechecking my bag to make sure that I have not forgotten something: that I have a new tape in the recorder, that the battery is still adequately charged, and that my tape recorder still works, even with the sand and saltwater that has blown inside despite all my efforts to seal it up in plastic storage bags bought during treasured trips to the U.S. commissary. Then, unable to justify dawdling any longer, and knowing that if I sit alone too long I will be accosted by one of the many young men roaming the outside edges of the beach, I stand up and start to wander nonchalantly along the edge of the water, peeking under the umbrellas and makeshift tents to find a woman of childbearing age with children.

Up ahead I notice two women in bathing suits sitting under an umbrella, chatting happily. A four-year-old boy is playing near the water in front of them with his ten-year-old cousin. And so I meet Sherifa and her *louza* (sister-in-law), Kareema, who lives next door to Sherifa. As Kareema explains in Tunisian Arabic, "(Sherifa) is my *mart khou* (the wife of my brother)."

"I am always over at her house. We eat together over there, or I sleep over there," she laughs. "I am always over there."

"She goes shopping with me in Tunis," Sherifa explains in Arabic. "She goes shopping with me in France. Where I go shopping she comes with me always. We are like sisters. I never had a sister and she never had a sister."

"We love each other a lot. We are always together. We live together!" exclaims Kareema.

As I discover later during the interview, however, Sherifa's *louza* is actually not a "true" sister-in-law (in strict biological kinship terms). "Sherifa's husband is my father's cousin," explains Kareema. "He is not my brother. But my father cared for him when he was growing up. He is like my brother. So we say I am her *louza* (sister-in-law)."

Not only does Sherifa live next door to her *louza*, Kareema, but her own home is part of a divided "kin complex" consisting of her husband's household and the households of four of her husband's brothers. "After I married I lived with my mother-in-law, and then she died," Sherifa explains.

"And where do you live now?" I ask.

"Over there," answers Kareema, pointing in the direction of some houses near the La Marsa beach. "Always in the house of her mother-in-law. Her mother-in-law's house is very big. So they broke it up after her death. Everyone now lives in a part—everyone has their own small apartment."

As a result, Sherifa sees most of her in-laws almost daily. On the particular day of my interview, a number of Sherifa's nieces and nephews (the children of her in-laws) were at the beach with her, as Kareema pointed out. "That one is the daughter of her brother-in-law (*bint silf*). And this one at the ocean," she points, "is her *bint silf*. And her *wuld silf* (son of her brother-in-law). The whole family is with us on the beach."

Sherifa does have one brother-in-law who lives in Bizerte. He comes to Tunis regularly to visit his brothers, so she usually sees him at least once a week.

However, although Sherifa lives in a world of her husband's kin—the ideal patrilocal Arab pattern—she continues to maintain strong ties to her natal family. She visits her parents and her married brother, who live together not far from her home in La Marsa, "*kul youm*" (every day). Since most of Sherifa's natal family has lived in La Marsa for many generations, she continues to see many of her relatives, who live nearby, frequently. "She is a *Marsawiyya* (from an original La Marsa family). Long long long back: her family, her father's family, her mother's family," explains Kareema.

Consequently Sherifa visits with four of her *khalet* (maternal aunts) two to three times a week. She has one other *khala* who is currently living in Rome; her aunt's husband works for the Tunisian embassy there. Despite the international distance, Sherifa's *khala* in Rome usually visits her family in Tunis a couple of times a year.

Sherifa also has five paternal uncles (*ammoum*) and three paternal aunts (*ammet*). However, she does not visit any of them. The schism with her father's kin is due, at least in part, to her choice of husband.

Kareema begins, "Well, she loved my brother, Abdelsalem. She was in love with him and everything. Her father told her, 'Choose someone from the family'—from his family. And Sherifa told him, 'I love him. I want to marry him.' So she went and got married and she was cut off from her relatives. And she had a son—this one," Kareema points to the four-year-old boy playing near us. "Her father didn't want to accept him. It's true. Her father said, 'Don't accept this one, he's not good. You should have someone a bit better.' But she loved him and took him."

Although Abdelsalem was not from Sherifa's family, like Sherifa his family considers themselves to be original *Marsawiyya,* families that have lived in the La Marsa area for generations. They are well-to-do farmers, owning not only a home near the beach but also farmland just on the outskirts of this northern suburb of Tunis. Abdelsalem has had little schooling, choosing instead to follow the family tradition of farming. Their household has a moderate income by Tunisian standards of approximately 250 dinars per month. However, they have significantly more assets than most of the women in the study. They own land, a house, a car, a television, a radio, a refrigerator, and a stove. They also have many animals: chickens, sheep, goats, cows, and donkeys. And a maid comes every other day to take care of the housework.

Whereas Abdelsalem had virtually no schooling, Sherifa has some secondary school education. She terminated her studies when she got married at age twenty, never holding a job. They had a son a year and a half later. Sherifa is now twenty-six and Abdelsalem is thirty-one, and they have been married six years.

Although Sherifa has a full and active visiting network of daily and weekly exchanges with seventeen households of kin, many of whom live right next door to her, she does not include a single neighbor or friend in the network. "I have neighbors but they are not friends. *'Aslama, bislama'* ('Hello, good-bye'), that's it. They don't come to me and I don't go to them. I don't like to socialize with neighbors," Sherifa states clearly. "I made only one friend. But my close relatives—I have many."

It is now five o'clock in the evening and we have been talking for at least two hours. The stifling heat of the day is slowly giving way to the refreshingly cool offshore breezes that make summer nights in Tunis so delightful. I thank Sherifa and Kareema for their time. We exchange addresses, for as I have discovered this is the only "payment" that most women will accept for the interview: a postcard from the United States. Then, settling into a quiet corner near the road, I sit patiently writing up my comments and notes about the interview, labeling my tapes, and listening for the puttering motor of Lorenz's moped.

DEFINING KINSHIP

Like Miriam's, Sherifa's network is typical of the most basic and central pattern of women's social ties in Tunis: a network centered around kin. Indeed, the idiom of kinship is so important that many women in my study would label ties with nonkin or more distant kin with more intimate kinship terms, as, for example, in the case of Sherifa's *louza*, Kareema. Given the loose and fluid structure of households, often close kin, distant relatives, and nonrelatives—particularly "adopted children"[1] such as Kareema's husband—become incorporated temporarily or permanently into the household by being given close kinship terms. Distinguishing biological kin from fictive kin was not always possible in my research, and perhaps not truly necessary since, biological or not, women considered these network members to be part of their kin group.

Marriage and kinship, however, do not necessarily guarantee a woman an entree into the social worlds and class of her kin. As Sherifa's story illustrates, certain kin or branches of the kin group may elect to withdraw from the visiting network, refusing to exchange visits, essentially breaking ties with kin considered of lower status or "not good enough."

The voluntary nature of kinship and visits with kin is also illustrated in Selwa's case. A thirty-year-old mother of three, Selwa, who studied hairdressing in secondary school, married a shoemaker with a sixth-grade education from the south of Tunis. She supplements her husband's limited income with her own home hairdressing business, and the two earn approximately 190 dinars a month. Selwa's modest income and working-class situation apparently are embarrassing to her upwardly mobile maternal uncles (*khouel*), so they do not visit.

"No, it's rare. We don't see each other often because they think they are 'bourgeois,'" Selwa answers in Arabic, electing, however, to use the French word "bourgeois" here. "They don't concern themselves with us."

"And I too, I don't like to go to them. If they're going to think like that, that's up to them. I don't go."

Significantly, since women (and their kin) select the relatives that they choose to visit, despite Arab ideals of patrilineality and patrilocal-

*A wealthy Arab villa
in the menzehs.*

ity, from the perspective of women in my study, kinship continues to be bilateral after marriage, with co-residence spread more or less equally between affinal and consanguineal kin.

THE KINSHIP NEIGHBORHOOD

Ideally and historically, the Arab family has been described as extended and patrilocal: After marriage women would live with their husband's kin, returning to visit their natal family only on special holidays and occasions. With the advent of industrialization and migration to urban areas, however, the extended household was predicted to disappear, being replaced instead by the more mobile nuclear household (Goode 1970). As Sherifa's case indicates, however, although nuclear households may indeed be on the rise in Tunis, most large and impersonal surveys and census data may be missing an important transformation in the Tunisian household: The extended household has simply "gone up" or "out," becoming instead the "extended street" or "extended apartment complex."

Sherifa, for example, initially lived with her mother-in-law and her brothers-in-law after her marriage: the ideal extended patrilocal pattern. Upon her mother-in-law's death (her father-in-law had died a few years earlier), the brothers then decided to split the large house into separate apartments for each married couple. This division had the outcome of accommodating the desires of each household for some financial and social independence while still maintaining the integrity of extended ties.

Although Sherifa now can manage her household budget and affairs (at least theoretically) independently of her husband's brothers, she still continues to live in a world of affinal kin, interacting with and assisting her neighbors (in-laws) on an almost daily basis. As she explained in her interview, if she runs short of food, she borrows from her *silfet* (sisters-in-law) and vice versa, and she often watches her sister-in-law's son (*wuld silfa*). If she needs transportation, her *louza*, Kareema, gives her a ride in her car, and if she needs advice it is Kareema she turns to. The two of them are as close "as sisters," going everywhere together, even to France. Since importation of foreign goods was extremely restricted during my first field trip (restrictions being slightly lowered on my return six years later), it was common for women in wealthier families to plan shopping trips abroad—particularly to France—to obtain desired foreign status-producing goods.

Significantly, however, despite Sherifa's intense daily interaction with her in-laws and her continued patrilocal residence, she very clearly continues to maintain close ties to her parents and brother. She visits her mother "every day," and if she needs someone to take care of her son, Bchir, whether she is going shopping, out for the evening to a wedding or social event, or even on a long trip, it is her mother who cares for him. When Sherifa falls sick, her mother cares for her; after the birth of Bchir, her mother was the one who helped out, staying in Sherifa's house for forty days.

Sherifa's strong and continuing ties with her own family are not unique. In my survey women showed a statistically significant preference (p < .007) for visiting *their own natal kin* rather than the predicted patrilineal pattern of ties to the husband's or affinal kin. Women reported regular visits to an average of 7.9 consanguineal kin-related households, in contrast to only 4.1 affinal relatives.[2]

Although these findings would seem to contradict much of the literature on the patrilineal Arab family in Tunisia and the Middle East, I suggest that to a large degree the notion of patrilineal Arab ties has been based on studies by men of the men's world in the Middle East. Although inheritance, property, and residence may (at least ideally and historically) be primarily dictated by ties through males, the assumption that Arab women's personal ties and social relations would automatically conform to this patrilineal ideal has never actually been investigated. An overwhelming majority of studies of Arab women show that after their marriages most women continue to maintain strong and intimate ties with their natal family, often relying on their own kin to defend and assist them in conflicts with their in-laws. Since visiting is a *choice* as well as an obligation, the women in my study reflect their continued love and attachment to their parents, brothers, sisters, grandparents, uncles, aunts, and cousins by selecting whom they will visit and how often.

This continued strong attachment to the woman's natal family, even when the woman lives with her husband's family, is illustrated in Nejiha's story. Like Sherifa, Nejiha lives with her husband's kin and has a large kin exclusive network of seventeen kin-related households. The network, however, is composed not only of her husband's relatives but also of her own natal kin. Thirty-seven-year-old Nejiha and her husband, Kareem, both come from original Tunis families. Nejiha studied up to the *sixième* (sixth grade) and worked at a hairdressing salon until her marriage to her husband, who was a cousin of the salon's owner. Kareem is somewhat more educated, having completed tenth grade. He currently works at a bank and earns a little more than 100 dinars a month.

The couple have two girls, ages seven and eleven, and live next door to all of Kareem's family in a row of villas dominating a side street in La Marsa. Consequently, Nejiha sees her in-laws "every day." Not only does Nejiha live in a kinship-based neighborhood, but her widowed father and three brothers all live next door to each other in a working-class Tunis neighborhood, Bab Souika. Nejiha generally visits her father and brothers once a week. Because several of her other relatives live near to her father or visit him frequently, she often visits with them, too.

"My father and brothers, we see each other once a week. . . . I see my cousin (*bint 'amm*) a lot because she lives next to my father. So whenever I go to see him I visit her."

"Do you see your maternal aunt (*khala*)?" I ask.

"At the time when I go to see my father and she's there," answers Nejiha. "Once every one to two weeks. She doesn't live far; in the same neighborhood."

"And your paternal uncle (*'amm*)?"

"He visits with my father every day, always."

"So perhaps when you are at your father's house . . . ," I interject.

"Yes, like that," Nejiha smiles. "When I go down to visit my father."

Kin not only live next door to each other, expanding in essence the extended Arab house into an extended Arab family street, but also sometimes expand vertically, into the extended family apartment building. Aya, for example is a thirty-two-year-old mother of two children. Educated up through secondary school, Aya worked in insurance before her marriage. However, since her marriage she has donned a formal veil (*hijab*) and now remains at home. Unlike Nejiha and Sherifa, however, she and her husband do not live with or near to any kin in their home on the outskirts of the suburb of Manouba. Yet, as she explains, speaking in French, she still manages to see her parents and her brothers in the nearby suburb of Megrine at least weekly.

"My brothers, they live with my mother, the three of them. You see, my father's house has three floors, ground floor, first floor—it's an apartment building."

"They all live in the same house . . . ," I interject.

"But each one lives in his own apartment," she explains.

"Each time you go there . . . ,"

"To my parents. I see them," Aya answers.

More than a quarter of the supposedly isolated nuclear households of the women in the survey were actually part of such extended kin-neighbor complexes.[3] These kin complexes function in many ways as larger extended households in which kin/neighbors exchange food, child care, and other services on a daily basis.

Soraya, a forty-year-old *Tunisoise* woman who grew up in Tunis, describes, in French, her childhood kin complex: "Everyone was there. We lived together, we grew up together with my paternal cousins. . . . We practically lived together. My father built his house facing my uncle. And the last uncle lived with his mother. He inherited her house."

Hence, although each family member resides physically in a separate nuclear household, socially and psychologically they still live with their extended family. One could, in fact, argue that the extended Arab household in Tunis has simply mutated outwards and upwards in accordance with new urban spatial realities.

Sherifa's, Soraya's, and Nejiha's co-residence experiences are far from atypical; the tendency to continue to live with or near kin is quite clear. Almost half of the women in my survey (44 percent) described living with or next door to kin. Underscoring their strong continuing interdependence on kin, like Sherifa, almost two-thirds (61.5 percent) of the women with kin exclusive networks either lived with or next door to kin, in comparison to a general survey co-residence rate of 44 percent (see Table A2.3 in Appendix 2). These high co-residence rates are similar to recent findings in studies of households and residence patterns in Algeria and Morocco.[4]

Guerraoui's (1996) excellent analysis of household structure in Fes suggests a very compelling explanation for the continued co-residence of kin, and especially the currently increasing pattern of nuclear households that includes one or two additional widowed or single kin-related adults. Given the economic insecurities of many households (difficulty in finding employment, the instability of many positions, and the irregularities of income for the self-employed) coupled with high housing costs, many households, and especially single and widowed members, find survival possible only by pooling together the incomes of several potential breadwinners. In this manner, not only does each household have more than one income to cover basic living costs, but should one income earner lose his or her job or become disabled or sick, there are still other wage earners in the household to continue supporting the group.

The practice of residing with or next door to kin does not merely maintain ties of assistance and support between kin who live near each other, however. As Nejiha's visits to her father and brothers illustrate, kin-neighborhood complexes often serve as a central meeting place where the extended family congregates and can visit with everyone at once, especially for women who do not live near kin.

Weekends, and particularly Sundays, are a favorite time for family get-togethers, which are typically held at the parents' house. Manil, for example, is a twenty-eight-year-old single woman who lives in a *foyer,* a student apartment that she shares with several other young unmarried students and working women. Manil has a university degree and works as a secretary for an international company in Tunis. Yet despite her seemingly "Westernized" lifestyle (unmarried, educated, living alone, and working), she makes the seventy-kilometer trip to visit her family in Bizerte every weekend.

"Do you visit your mother?" I ask.

"Yes," she replies in excellent French, "every weekend, every weekend. Saturday, Sunday, holidays. I'm the one who goes there."

"And your married sisters, do you visit them?"

"In principle we meet each other at my parents' house," she replies. "Everyone gets together on Sunday, the whole family reunites on Sunday in order to spend the day together."

Although most weekly family get-togethers involve kin who live in Tunis, as Manil's case illustrates, even when kin live far away, visiting and its concomitant support and exchange still continue.

MIGRATION AND LONG-DISTANCE VISITS

As I have described elsewhere (Holmes-Eber 1997a, 1997b), for the women in this study, ties to extended kin living outside of Tunis in the hometown or even overseas in Europe or the Arab States persist up to several generations after migration. Although *Tunisoise* women did visit significantly more kin living in Tunis than migrant women did, migrant women's networks included twice as many households outside of the capital city. Indeed, on the average approximately 40 percent of the kin-related households in migrant women's networks were more than fifty kilometers away from Tunis.

In contrast to daily or weekly visits to kin living nearby in Tunis, visits to relatives outside of Tunis were typically less frequent but lasted much longer. Many of the migrant women in my study preferred visiting their hometown and extended families, if they could afford it, for at least several weeks or months each year, especially during vacations and holidays. Summer and holiday visits to the hometown often become enlarged family get-togethers where kin who have been dispersed all over the country, or even overseas, return to spend time with one another, as Fauzia's story illustrates.

Fauzia is a forty-nine-year-old mother of three boys and one girl ranging in age from eleven to twenty-three. At our first meeting in 1986 Fauzia was living with all of her four children, her husband, and her brother-in-law. Her oldest daughter, Rania, who was engaged at the time to a coworker at her job at the post office, got married two years later. They moved into an apartment around the corner, where she, her new husband, and their baby were living during the follow-up study in 1993.

Fauzia and Mehdi, her husband, come from a coastal town in the Sahelian region about a four-hour drive from Tunis. Fauzia has no education and has never worked, whereas Mehdi has a French university degree and holds a position in the Tunisian government. They are fairly well off, living on an income of 250 dinars or more a month excluding their daughter Rania's income (which she used for her own expenses and dowry).

Unlike Sherifa or Nejiha, Fauzia has no close kin living in Tunis, except for her brother-in-law, who lives with them. Most of Fauzia's family lives far away in neighboring towns in the Sahel. Her mother and paternal aunt and one sister live in a small coastal town, and her second sister and three sisters-in-law live nearby in Monastir. One of Fauzia's brothers lives approximately a hundred kilometers farther south of Monastir in Sfax. Her two older brothers emigrated to Europe, one to France and the other to Sweden.

Yet despite Fauzia's distance from her extended kin, every summer she goes to her hometown in Monastir for at least a month or two to enjoy the ocean and to visit with family. Fauzia is not the only migrant to return each year to Monastir. Relatives scattered throughout the country and even in Europe return to spend their vacations in their hometown, resulting in an annual family reunion. As she explains shyly to me in Tunisian Arabic, "I see my relatives in Monastir when

A girl from the south of Tunisia wearing a Berber shawl.

I go down there. In the summer I leave. Every year in the summer I go, myself and the children. The wife of my brother—the one in France— she comes. There is the wife of my other brother in Sfax. Everyone. The Swedish woman [married to her third brother and living in Sweden] comes."

Weddings and other social occasions also bring Fauzia's kin group together. "I have lots of paternal cousins. I see them at celebrations, at weddings or things. When I go there to the Sahel. Or if they're in Tunis. We meet at special occasions. The relatives are there."

Like summer vacations, family celebrations serve as an opportunity to unite kin who are dispersed throughout the country and even overseas. At her daughter Rania's engagement party, for example, not only did Fauzia's relatives come up from Monastir, but her brothers flew back from Europe, and an aunt in Canada returned to share in the celebrations.

As Fauzia's case demonstrates, even migration overseas does not necessarily end visiting exchanges between kin. Sherifa, too, mentions not only a brother-in-law who returns regularly from Bizerte to visit but also an aunt who comes once or twice a year from Rome.

KIN EXCLUSIVE NETWORKS AND MIGRATION

Not all migrants, however, can afford to make the expensive trip back home each summer, as Miriam's story in Chapter 4 illustrates. Whether the woman is a migrant is an important dividing factor for women with kin exclusive networks. Whereas all but one of the *Tunisoise* women, like Sherifa, had at least a few years of high school or professional school training, like Miriam, most of the migrant women with kin exclusive networks never completed sixth grade.

These differences in education between the migrant and *Tunisiose* women are also reflected in the occupations and education of the women's husbands. Whereas only two of the eight migrant women's husbands had studied past the sixth grade, all but one of the *Tunisoise* husbands (Sherifa's husband) had at least a secondary professional or high school education. Correspondingly, the majority of the migrant women's husbands, like Sami, tended to hold low-skilled and unreliable positions. In contrast, most of the *Tunisoise* women's husbands held professional positions or worked for the government.

As in Miriam's case, all of the migrant women with kin exclusive networks married kin, and most (85 percent) married someone from the hometown. In contrast, only one of the *Tunisioise* women married endogamously. Interestingly, however, five of the *Tunisoise* women married men from Tunis. Regional endogamy (84.6 percent) is extremely high for women with kin exclusive networks, regardless of whether the woman is a migrant.

These figures present pictures of two distinct groups of women with kin exclusive networks. On the one hand, there are the *Tunisoise* women, generally well educated and married to men who hold respectable, stable positions, often with the government. Perhaps reflecting their higher education, these women marry outside of the kin group but hold onto class lines, still marrying *Tunisoise* men. On the other hand are the migrant women and their husbands, who tend to have a limited education and whose jobs most typically can be characterized as unskilled manual labor.

Migrant women with kin exclusive networks clearly focus all of their resources within one kin group, socializing almost exclusively with kin, marrying kin, and selecting spouses from their region of origin. In contrast, *Tunisoise* women's kin exclusive networks reflect a somewhat different strategy. Descendants of the original and "true" Tunis families, these women and their kin look down upon the "*arrivistes*," as Soraya, a forty-six-year-old woman from an old *Tunisoise* family, once pejoratively referred to them.

Jemila Belhedi, a migrant unmarried university student, described the friction between these original Tunis families and the new generation of migrants: "The *Tunisoises* hold themselves too much as a superior people. Even if they are very kind, even if they are very modest, they cannot forget that they belong to a certain family. The *Tunisoises* live too much '*en famille*' (as a family). They truly have very intimate relations with each other."

These families see the old class system as their primary strategy for success: creating and maintaining ties almost exclusively with other old Tunis families. Instead of practicing kin endogamy, which tends to concentrate the kin and resources among a small group, these *Tunisoise* women and their families practice regional endogamy, allying themselves with a much larger network of kin from a similar social class and background. Hence, although they continue to invest in the kin group, excluding outsiders from their networks, by creating marital alliances with other Tunis families they spread their social and resource base much more widely, seeking to maximize connections with kin placed in advantageous positions.

It is not surprising, then, that Sherifa faced immense pressure to marry "someone better" when she chose a farmer for her husband. Although he too came from a well-established, landed family, his kin were not considered an advantageous match for Sherifa's parents, who could list an embassy wife in Rome (Sherifa's *khala*) as part of their network. The consequence of her choice was quite severe for a woman who centered her social network and ties around kin: a complete rupture of ties with her father's kin, her '*ammet* and '*ammoum*.

Although kinship forms the backbone of all women's networks, as Nura's story in Chapter 6 illustrates, for many women the neighborhood, whether composed of kin or unrelated households, often plays a significant role in women's survival strategies and network styles.

Notes

1. Legal adoption is not practiced among Muslims. However, many households in Tunis end up, in practice, caring for other children (particularly orphaned relatives). Typically these children assume "adoptive" intimate kinship terms such as "brother" or "sister," "son" or "daughter," rather than their actual tie of, say, "cousin."

2. These figures exclude ten women who were married to relatives. In these cases, of course, the woman's relatives were also her husband's relatives, so that making the distinction between affinal and consanguineal kin was not possible.

3. These figures are probably low because I never directly asked women if they lived next door to kin. In my survey, I merely asked women where people in their network lived, which led a number of them to volunteer the information that they lived next door to each other.

4. Adel (1996) reports that although nuclear households in Algeria have increased slightly, cohabitation with kin continues to constitute almost one-third of all Algerian households. Similarly, Guerraoui (1996) reports a rate of 30.3 percent for households cohabiting with kin in Fez, Morocco. And the Royaume du Maroc (1996) found in a 1995 National Survey of the Family that 37.4 percent of the households in rural areas included extended kin and an only very slightly lower percentage, 34.7 percent, of urban households were composed of extended kin. Furthermore, the Morocco survey found that a meaningful percentage of households resided near and next door to kin. Thirty-two percent of urban households lived in the same building as kin, 12.8 percent lived in contiguous structures, and 44.5 percent lived in the same quarter (Royaume du Maroc, 1996).

6

Intimate Economies:
Nura's Neighbor Network

It is still early, not quite ten A.M., and the harsh July sun has not quite completely burned off a light morning fog. The long sandy beach is still quiet, not yet filled up with the bright umbrellas and Tunisian blankets, the cries of the *kakaweeat* sellers, and the delighted screams of the children as they run in and out of the water. This early in the morning the tents and umbrellas and blankets are spread rather far apart, and so I have a few minutes of walking to catch my breath and prepare my introduction.

Ahead of me is a large group of women, dressed in simple patterned cotton dresses and skirts, heads covered with brightly colored scarves, sitting barefooted on several faded woolen Tunisian blankets. At least a dozen small children in shorts and summer dresses are seated in between their mothers or running around the blankets. I stop in front of their blanket.

"*Aslama* . . ." I begin.

"*Bifathl*," (Please) answers a strong-boned, dark-haired woman, dressed in a nice patterned summer dress. And so I meet Nura and her neighbors.

As the women see my blonde hair and hear my American-accented Tunisian Arabic, there are cries of laughter and astonishment. Most foreigners they have seen speak only French or perhaps, rarely, standard Arabic, if they speak any of Tunisia's languages. Since Nura and her neighbors only speak Tunisian Arabic, this is certainly an unexpected opportunity to meet one of these strangers. Almost immediately I am met with a barrage of three, four, five voices asking all at once: *"Mineenik?"* (Where are you from?); *"Keef 'alemt litkelim l'arabeea?"* (How did you learn to speak Arabic?); *"Inti tadrass?"* (Are you studying?); *"M'arissa littouwensa?"* (Are you married to a Tunisian?).

Then as I answer, as in most of my interviews, there is more laughter, and smiles. A couple of the women seem a little uncomfortable, so Nura, voluble, lively, and clearly confident, takes charge.

"'Aqad, 'aqad!" (Sit down, sit down), she motions to a spot next to her on the blanket. *"Esh taheb t'arif?"* (What would you like to know?) she asks, and the interview begins.

Nura lives in Bab el Khathra, a poor and working-class neighborhood centered on one of the ancient gates, or *Babs,* that once permitted entrance into the original Arab-walled city, or *medina.* She lives in an apartment along with her brother-in-law (*silf*), her husband, Hamid, their three children, and (most of the time) Hamid's widowed mother. "I generally have my mother-in-law, but sometimes she goes over to stay with her daughter. Then I visit her. If she is staying over there, I go to visit her. But usually, I have her here."

The apartment that they rent is part of an old Arab house, made up of a series of unconnected rooms on three levels, all centered around a communal courtyard. Originally built for large extended families that shared the courtyard for household tasks such as washing, food preparation, and sanitation, Nura's building, like many of the former stately Arab houses in Tunis, has been divided up into residences for nine unrelated families. "We have neighbors. It's an Arab house. And everyone [she points to the other women sitting on the blankets around her at the beach], we all live like this—together. I have my own home, and they, [nods toward neighbors]—eight of us all together—all of them have their own home."

Because of their proximity and the communal nature of the central courtyard, Nura is close friends with her neighbors, visiting with and in-

Women wearing gelabias on a visit with their children.

teracting with them "every day." When I ask Nura which of her neighbors she visits, she replies, "Ayza," pointing to the woman next to her. "She is like a sister to me."

"And do you have any other neighbors that you know well?"

"There are some like this one," Nura smiles at another one of the women sitting next to her, "a long time. But there are some new ones living with us. They move in and they go. There are three neighbors. We have stayed together from the beginning. For twenty-five years my husband has been in this house. His mother and father, too."

Nura's husband, Hamid, was born in the south of Tunisia, in Matmata, not far from Nura's family's hometown of Hamma. When he was a child his parents moved to Tunis and settled into the Arab house that, later, became Nura's home after her marriage. Nura, who has four years of schooling and has never worked outside of the home, met Hamid through her neighbor.

"His sister was our neighbor," she explains.

"And did you choose him or did someone else choose him for you?" I ask.

"The whole family chose him," she replies.

Nura explains that she and Hamid have been married ten years. Over the years Hamid, who only went to school until the *sixième* (sixth grade), has worked in construction and as a bus driver. Their total household income, including the contributions from Hamid's brother who is also living with them, is 200 dinars a month, a moderate income by Tunisian standards.

Although Nura lives with her husband's family, her primary network ties continue to be with her own kin. Although she occasionally visits Hamid's sister in Manouba (her old neighborhood), she does not visit any of his other relatives except at holidays (*mounesibet*). In contrast, she explains, "I see my brothers and sisters once or twice a week. I always see them because I go to my mother's house and they live over there, near my mother. . . . I visit my mother every week."

Nura's extended kin network is, in fact, quite large. "The whole family is in Manouba (a middle-class, suburb)," she explains. And so she "always visits" her three uncles (*khouel*, mother's brothers) and two of her mother's sisters (*khalet*), seeing them at least once a month.

Nura has more cousins and children of her cousins than she cares to count. "My aunts and uncles have children and they are married with their own children. Some of them [aunts and uncles] have seven kids and there are some who have eight and some who have six and some who have five." Although she sees most of her cousins on holidays and special occasions, she has one special maternal cousin who lives near her in Hay elKhathra that she visits regularly: "My *bint khal* who lives in Hay elKhathra, I always see her. Once a month or every two months, when there is a special occasion, I go."

As I wind up the interview, asking questions about assistance and sharing patterns in the network, it is clear that Nura feels very close to her natal family. In addition to visiting her parents every Sunday, she goes to them for advice and help. If she falls ill, it is Nura's sister, not her mother-in-law, who cares for her. And if she needs to borrow money, she turns to her sister.

From Nura's point of view her *hmet* (mother-in-law), who lives with them at least part of the year, is not much help at all. Nura insists that she does the wash, the cooking, the dishes, the shopping, and the housework all alone. In fact, she admits, with a giggle in front of her neighbors, that she does not get along well with her mother-in-law—a comment that her neighbors do not dispute.

We have been talking for an hour and a half and it is almost noon. Not wanting Nura and her neighbors to feel obliged to offer me lunch, I thank them for the interview and pack up my bag, looking for a shady spot to write up my notes about the interview, before heading out once again across the hot sand to peer under the suddenly numerous umbrellas and makeshift tents and ask once more, *"Aslama, n'amal bahath . . ."*

THE NEIGHBOR NETWORK

Like Sherifa and Miriam, the majority of Nura's network (sixteen households) consists of kin, who are overwhelmingly from Nura's natal and mother's family. Nura does, however, reside in a semi-extended patrilineal household with her brother-in-law and—for much of the year—her mother-in-law. Yet unlike Sherifa and Miriam, in addition to this central core of kin, Nura's network includes a clique of eight neighbors that she sees "every day," some of whom she has known since she moved in with her in-laws ten years previously. As is evidenced by Nura's trip to the beach with her neighbors the day of my interview, Nura's neighbors form a cohesive group of women who not only socialize and help each other out with the practical daily domestic activities but also enjoy each other's company enough to take outings together.

Nura's social and visiting ties are typical of the network type I have categorized as the "neighbor network." Like both the "kin exclusive network" and the "friendship pattern," neighbor networks are typically dominated by kin, with a mean number of twelve kin-related households in the network (see Table A2.1, Appendix 2). The distinguishing feature of neighbor networks, however, is that in addition to their regular and often frequent visits with kin, these woman rely on a close network of five to six neighbors who assist each other on a daily basis.

In my survey almost two-thirds of the women with neighbor networks, like Nura, have had fewer than six years of schooling. Four women did continue past primary school, but in all cases these women continued on to a trade school to learn such skills as sewing or hairdressing.

Although more than half of the women had worked prior to their marriage, none of the women with neighbor networks were currently employed outside of the home, probably because most of them had held unskilled, low-status positions prior to their marriage: in factories, as a migrant worker to Germany, and as a hairdresser. However, although none of the women were currently working in the formal economy, four women were earning some income from enterprises inside their homes. One woman had set up a home-based business as a hairdresser for her friends, neighbors, and relatives; two sold homemade knitting and handicrafts through businesses in the *souks;* and the fourth sewed clothes on consignment for her relatives and neighbors.

The decision for these women to remain in the home after marriage reflected their strong valuation of women's place in the home rather than the lack of financial need for the women to work. Even with the supplemental income that the women made in their home businesses, household incomes for these women were the lowest for all the women in my study, averaging approximately 160 dinars per month.

In fact, most of the women lived in a very precarious financial situation. Two women, Mounia and Douzha, were widows with young children. Only Fauzia's husband held a skilled, stable position in the government. Virtually all of the other women's husbands were either self-employed—as a shoemaker, a vegetable seller, a shopkeeper, and an artisan in the *souks*—or held unskilled jobs: as a bus driver (Hamid), a mechanic, in the national guard, as a waiter, and as a farm laborer.

Significantly, the overwhelming majority (83 percent) of women with "neighbor networks" are first- or second- generation migrants to Tunis, as are their husbands. As Nura's case exemplifies, the picture one develops of women with neighbor networks is of an unskilled or manually skilled migrant woman and her husband, both with limited education, whose social world revolves around kin and the neighbors that she relies on for daily support and assistance, protecting her against the financial insecurities of her precarious economic situation. These women and their lively, noisy neighborhood networks seem very much like the *baldi* women described in other urban areas of the Middle East such as Cairo and Istanbul.

NEIGHBORHOODS AND NETWORKS

Although not all women socialize with their neighbors, for many of the women who live in the poorer working-class quarters of Tunis, the *quartiers populaires*, neighbors become an essential part of daily life and survival. Women with neighbor networks often speak of each other and treat each other like kin, even using kinship terms to describe the relationship. Nura, for example, referred to her neighbor, Ayza, as "like a sister."

These kinship terms are more than just a sign of affection. For many women with neighbor networks such as Selwa, a thirty-year-old migrant woman who had her own hairdressing business in her home, the choice of kin terms reflects a real-life intimacy and intense daily interaction with her neighbors that echoes ties with "real" kin. Selwa had just moved from her neighborhood in Le Bardo and spoke with great affection of her former neighbors: "We call ourselves sisters. They are like my sisters. We would eat together, drink a coffee in the afternoon together. We would go out together in the car, we would take our kids with us. We're really close friends, really close."

In Selwa's case, many of her close neighbors were also her clients, who enjoyed the opportunity to have their hair done while catching up on the neighborhood gossip in Selwa's hairdressing salon in her house.

The importance of kinshiplike support and intimacy with their neighbors for women with neighbor networks is also echoed in an interview with Douzha, a twenty-seven-year-old widow. Like Nura, Douzha, a migrant woman with only a sixth-grade education, had come to the beach for the day with her neighbors, who all lived in separate houses in a housing project, or *hay*. The project was part of a government program to provide affordable housing to the poor, and each month Douzha paid twenty dinars toward its purchase. Although young, she had been widowed five years before, just before the birth of her second child, and was trying to make a living on a minimal pension of only sixty dinars a month from the factory where her husband had worked. She survived through the support and assistance of her neighbors and her family, including an unmarried uncle, *khal*, who was currently living with her.

Women shopping together in an open air market. Note that modesty of dress applies to men (who are covered in black burnous) as well as women (in white sifsarees).

The use of kinship (and visiting) as a metaphor for the intimate ties between Douzha's neighbors was echoed in her neighbor Kauther's description of their relationship: "We sit together. We drink tea. We eat together, we talk to each other. Everything together. We are family. We live together."

Given Douzha's precarious financial situation (and that of her neighbors, who were not much better off), neighborly assistance such as sharing food with each other when the cupboard was low (or bare) was an important part of the neighborhood's ethic. Douzha's neighbors helped each other out in many other ways that one would expect from kin: baby-sitting each other's children, sharing food, acting as escorts to each other when they would go out shopping or to the *hammam* (an important service for Douzha, who had no husband to escort her and protect her honor), and even assisting in preparing and contributing food and other goods for important celebrations such as Douzha's son's *tahour* (circumcision party), which she had celebrated just a month before.

Perhaps it is not surprising that the line between kin and neighbors is so thin for these women. Considering that for over half of the women in my survey, kin *were* neighbors, extending kinlike ties of support and intimacy to those living next door would fit naturally into the social fabric of many women's daily lives.

Not all Tunisian women include neighbors in their networks, however. Many of the women I interviewed, like Sherifa, stated that they did not like to socialize with their neighbors, describing the relationship as a formal one of mere greeting, "*Aslama bislama*" (hello, good-bye) when they would meet. Just as membership of kin in the visiting network is based to some degree on a woman's personal choice, so too is the inclusion of neighbors in the network, as illustrated by the Belhedis' neighborhood.

The Belhedi family, who had become my adopted family while we lived in Tunisia, lived on a quiet, narrow side street in the middle-class suburb of Megrine. The street had sprung up in the 1960s, and its modest new "French style" square cement block villas, each with a walled garden behind it, had appealed to the new upwardly mobile generation of government employees, many of whom had now lived on the street for twenty years or more. Unlike some of the older, original Tunis communities where housing had originally accommodated large extended families, this street was clearly designed for individual, separated households. Correspondingly, each of the households that I visited on this street was unrelated to its neighbors.

Despite the physical separation and lack of kinship ties between the houses on the street, however, over the many years of residing in a community of similarly well-to-do and well-connected government employees, several ties between neighbors had sprung up. Interestingly, however, rather than forming a cohesive group of neighbors, a clique formed on the street, based on region of origin: the coastal area of Tunisia called the Sahel.

This clique consisted of Zohra Belhedi, whose family came from the Sahel; Fauzia, her next-door neighbor, who was born in a community less than thirty kilometers away from Zohra's family; Soumaya, a Sfaxian woman (Sfax is at the southern end of the Sahel); and Mounia, a widowed woman who lived directly across the street from

Fauzia and Zohra and whose family originated from the Kerkenna Islands off of Sfax.

Significantly, two *Tunisoise* women living on the street did not participate in this clique: Samia, who lived next door to Zohra, and Soraya, who lived on the corner of the street. Indeed, I came to know Samia and Soraya, not through Zohra but through Zohra's son Sami. In the evening after work, or on the weekends, Sami would sometimes drop by our apartment in his newly purchased BMW, with Samia's daughters, Lilia and Lena, who were studying at the university, and we would take trips out to the cool hilltop town of Sidi Bou Said together.

I did not meet Soraya until almost nine months into my fieldwork, although Lorenz had met her and her family the first week we arrived in Tunis. During my visits to the Belhedis, Sami would often take off to a café with Lorenz and a number of the neighboring young men, including Soraya's twenty-five-year-old son, Mehdi. As Sami's significantly different social ties illustrate, women's and men's networks are often quite separate and distinct and do not necessarily coincide.

Unfortunately, as a woman, I could not collect comprehensive data on men's networks, which would have provided a fascinating comparison to my current study. Most of the information I have is anecdotal, based on comments made by my husband, Lorenz, or from those brief instances when I could observe men's network interactions (as, for example, when Lorenz's male friends would stop by to visit).

The regional nature of the Belhedis' neighborhood clique was underscored at Fauzia's daughter Rania's engagement celebration, or *fetiha*. Although the celebration was held in the neighborhood, in the garden behind Fauzia's house, the *Tunisoise* neighbors—Soraya, Samia, and Samia's daughters, Lilia and Lena—did not attend. In contrast, Mounia and her Sfaxian friend Soumaya played central roles in assisting Fauzia during the festivities, and Zohra, her daughter Jemila, and I were all invited.

For days before the celebration at the beginning of July, Fauzia (Rania's mother), Mounia (her widowed neighbor), and Fauzia's maid spent many exhausting hours in their hot summer kitchen preparing elaborate and expensive Tunisian cakes for the *fetiha*. On the night of the engagement party, Mounia, who lived directly across the street, converted her garage into a second kitchen for the occasion. Using a second refrigerator she had stored in the garage and several tables, she, Soumaya (the Sfaxian neighbor), and Fauzia set up tray upon tray of expensive cakes and sodas and then carried them across the street to be served to the hundred or so guests at Fauzia's house.

The music from the band's loud microphones blared cheerfully into the neighboring houses of Soraya and Samia until four o'clock in the morning, seemingly totally unconcerned about their absence from the festivities.

INTIMATE ECONOMIES: DAILY EXCHANGE AND THE INFORMAL SOCIAL SECURITY SYSTEM

Although Tunisian women visit for many occasions, ranging from the weekly Sunday visit to religious holidays and weddings, it is the simple, informal daily drop-in that forms the backbone of most women's day-to-day social life. During the weekday, neighbors, kin, and friends often stop by unannounced to chat, to visit, to lend a helping hand, to ask a favor, or just simply to say hello. Sometimes drop-ins are merely an opportunity to socialize, to take a break from washing tubs full of clothes by hand or rinsing bugs out of the bags of chickpeas and sprigs of parsley bought in the market that morning. Yet often enough, drop-ins have a specific purpose, whether overt or covert—perhaps to borrow a cup of tea or flour, to ask if the neighbor would mind watching the baby for a few minutes, and, frequently, to transfer information rapidly and personally in a country where the television and newspapers only report government-approved information[1] and telephones—although rapidly spreading with the arrival of cellular technology in the past few years—still are primarily accessible only to the well-to-do and to those who have the correct government connections. As my drop-ins to Najet's house and her cousin's house illustrate, these simple, informal, and typically unannounced visits are one of the primary ways that women disseminate information and trade assistance and services on a day-to-day basis.

At one-thirty, after a morning shopping in the souks, I decided to drop by and see if Najet was home. Najet's house, a modest, two-story concrete

house, was squeezed in between a row of similarly square, drab construc-
tions on a narrow, hilly street at the edge of the medina (one of the working-
class Tunis quarters).

Shapely, raven-haired, in a form-fitting knit red dress, twenty-six-year-
old Najet appeared at the door, alongside her mother and her married sis-
ter Ruaida, who lived next door and was also "dropping in" to visit her par-
ents. I entered the formal living room at the front of the house to find
Najet's father stretched out on the long wooden Tunisian bench, a large
white patch covering his eye and much of his face.

There had been an accident on the construction site where Najet's father
worked, Ruaida explained as she eased her rotund figure onto a nearby
couch and returned to her knitting. As their tense, silent faces revealed, the
injury was serious; Najet's father might not be returning to work for several
weeks. Since her father was self-employed and, therefore, fell outside of the
few government insurance programs, this meant that not only would the
family have to pay for the medical bills, they would be without an income
until Najet's father recovered. After being fed, despite my protestations, a
lunch of cold spaghetti, cold couscous with greens, a red-sauced salad, and
nectarines, Najet and I strolled off arm in arm to drop in on her cousin's
house, several twists and turns away tucked in a quiet cul-de-sac of the
medina. Najet's maternal aunt (khala) opened the ancient, metal-studded
wooden door wearing a housecoat, followed quickly by Emira, Najet's
cousin (bint khala), also wearing a housecoat over jeans and a sweatshirt.
The reason for the housecoats became apparent as we walked down the cold
flagstone corridor into the aging traditional Arab-style home, centered on
an open-aired palm-treed courtyard, that probably in warmer months was
a cool respite from the summer heat. Now it emanated the damp chill that
pervaded most older homes in Tunis in the grey rainy winter months, tem-
pered only briefly by small pockets of heat radiating from the kerosene, elec-
tric, and charcoal heaters around which everyone huddled red-nosed and
chapped-handed, waiting for warmer days.

We were then escorted into the sitting room, while Emira went to make
tea, coming back with four tall, slender glasses along with a bowl of jam
and some packaged cookies. Najet's aunt concernedly asked about the con-
dition of Najet's father—how he was doing after the accident, what the
doctors had said, if they needed anything—and then left. The conversation,

punctuated by the dramatic exclamations from an Egyptian soap opera on the television in the background, soon shifted to clothes and their prices; the costs of various rings Emira's fiancé was considering buying; and the problems that had resulted from Emira's request to celebrate the European New Year (Reveillon) with her fiancé, to which her family was vehemently opposed.

Feirouth, Emira's half-sister from a previous marriage of her father, suddenly dropped by with her six-month-old son. Quickly kissing all our cheeks, she animatedly launched into a discussion about the price of wool she wanted to buy for an embroidery pattern for a sweater. She then left the baby with us and went off to shop for the wool.

Since it was now four-thirty, I too decided to leave. Najet walked me to the main souk (market) street and we kissed good-bye while she returned to her cousin's house to visit a little longer.

My visits to these two homes lasted only three hours, and yet during this brief period I observed three other drop-ins: Ruaida was visiting her parents, Najet visited her cousin and aunt, and Feirouth stopped by briefly to visit and leave her baby with her mother and half-sister. Each drop-in was an informal affair. Hostesses greeted their guests in housecoats, simple foods such as cold left-over spaghetti and couscous or dried packaged biscuits and jam were offered, and the guests made themselves at home, knitting sweaters, dropping off a baby, and chatting with the television on in the background.

However, although informal and casual, these visits were far from frivolous, insignificant social calls. Much important social and economic information relating to the management of household affairs was exchanged. First, Najet carried tidings of her father's accident and condition to her aunt and cousin, playing an important role in mobilizing her family's kin network for support and assistance during the coming weeks of no income. Second, the three cousins discussed prices of various goods such as clothing, wool, and jewelry. Since goods are bargained for in the *souks*, knowledge of the fair going rate for various commodities is important if a good deal is to be closed. And finally, Najet and Emira analyzed the problems of appropriate social behavior with Emira's future husband, centering on the conflict surrounding Emira's desire to celebrate the European New Year with her fiancé (of which Emira's parents clearly disapproved). Since Najet's parents were violently opposed to her marrying her current boyfriend (a student whom Najet had been secretly dating for the past two years), her cousin's success—or failure—in convincing her parents to take a liberal view of dating and marriage would set a precedent for Najet. Information was not the only item exchanged in these drop-ins, however. Feirouth's main purpose for dropping in was to leave the baby while she shopped for wool for the baby outfit she was knitting. And Ruaida's primary reason for visiting was to assist her mother in caring for her injured father, as well as to help in receiving and hosting visitors who might be stopping by to offer their support.

One of the most significant ways in which women—and particularly neighbors and kin—assist each other is by watching each other's children. Although Tunis has seen the growth of part-time nursery schools for young children, full-time day care centers are hard to locate and extremely expensive. Paying a baby sitter to watch one's child for a few hours is considered a foreign practice. Although women with the financial means will hire a full- or part-time maid to care for the children and clean the house, never once during my research and trips to Tunisia have I ever known a family to actually hire a baby sitter for an afternoon or evening. Instead, child care, like food, is considered a social commodity that is shared with those in need.

For example, Aya, a thirty-year-old mother of two children ages eight and five, regularly leaves her children with her friend who lives next door. "I see her every day. Sometimes if I have to go to downtown Tunis, I leave my children with her. And she also—sometimes she sleeps over at my house because her husband works in customs. Sometimes he works at night. She prefers that she is at my house. Also if she is a little sick she stays with me."

As Aya's case illustrates, close friends and neighbors care not only for each other's children but also for one another, helping out when they are sick or traveling together when they do not have an escort. Given the cultural expectation that honorable women do not travel alone in Tunisia, escorting one's friend was an important service that neighbors frequently provided one another.

Not only do women drop in to exchange information and child care, but, especially in the case of neighbors, they often drop by to borrow or share food. Sharing food or staples is very common, helping to tide women over when they run short or must entertain guests. Because of the extremely limited amount of frozen, canned, or prepared goods, and the lack of refrigeration in many homes, women in Tunis usually shop for food daily at the many small local vendors, or perhaps in the large markets if they are nearby.

Although a few corner vendors may stay open until seven or eight o'clock in the evening, selling baguettes, tea, pasteurized milk, and cigarettes, most vendors are closed by early evening and over the noon hour. As a result, running short of food, particularly when unexpected guests arrive, is a frequent problem for most women, as Zohra Belhedi explains in French. "In the evening, in an emergency. . . . If there is a need—for example—my neighbors are looking for a little flour or bread. Myself too. If I need to make a cake—I'm having guests and I don't have any flour or sugar—I go to my neighbor."

In Tunisia one does not actually "loan" food, a concept alien to Arab principles of hospitality. Rather, food is given and shared with all who are in need, with the expectation that at a later date the favor will be reciprocated.

Not only do women exchange goods and services and information on a daily basis through their constant drop-ins to relatives and neighbors, but they also provide more extended assistance to needy members of the network, through the practice of long-term visits.

HOUSING ARRANGEMENTS AND LONG-TERM VISITS

Probably one of the most important ways that women help each other, and especially their kin, is by providing lodging, food, and economic assistance through a very interesting system of rotating visits. During long-term visits, visitors take up temporary residence in their relatives' or friends' homes for several months at a time. Sometimes these visitors have permanent residences elsewhere, and perhaps because of the long distances traveled simply want to visit awhile. Yet a significant portion of these visitors have no permanent home, moving from relative to relative so that the burden of their support is shared evenly among kin.

This is a particularly common pattern among widows, who rotate their visits among their children, a phenomenon I observed so often that I referred to them in my field notes as "floating widows." Nura, for example, mentions her mother-in-law, who lives part of the year with her husband's sister and the rest of the time with Nura and her husband and her brother-in-law. Likewise Selwa, a migrant woman who had her own home hairdressing business to supplement her husband's modest income as a shoemaker, shares the burden and cost of caring for her widowed mother with her siblings: "Since my father died, my mother stays with us. Sometimes my mother stays with me, sometimes my sister has her, sometimes my brother has her. Wherever, every time when she changes places I go to visit her, to whomever has her, you understand? Because she can't stay at home alone. She's an old woman, she can't."

And Samia, the *Tunisoise* neighbor of Zohra Belhedi, describes her widowed cousin: "You have three cousins in Manouba, one in Radis, one in Tunis." I am trying to sort out Samia's kinship ties, a particularly complicated topic since not only did Samia marry her *wuld 'amm*, but her husband's father married Samia's mother's sister (*khala*). "That makes . . ."

"Five," Samia answers. "The sixth cousin, she is always at her daughters' homes because her husband is dead. So she doesn't have a fixed place."

"So she lives with her family?" I ask.

"With her daughters, her children. She doesn't have a fixed home."

Like widows, orphaned children are sent to visit various relatives so that the entire kin group cooperates in raising them. For example, forty-one-year-old Mounia (Zohra's widowed neighbor from Kerkenna) was taking care of one of her teenage half-sisters, Manil, when I interviewed her in the summer. Her father had married six times (Mounia was from his first wife), wedding his sixth wife after Manil's mother died. He died soon thereafter, leaving three orphaned half-brothers and three half-sisters.

"This is one of my half-sisters," Mounia points to Manil. "Then there is her younger sister, and another married sister who's older than them and lives in Sfax. The younger one is staying with my brother in Germany. From there she comes to visit me and then it will be my turn to have her. I have her sister now."

Sometimes children are sent to visit their relatives (particularly grandparents) for a period of time if their parents are in a difficult financial or personal situation. For example, Hannan, a highly educated working woman (see Chapter 7), was pregnant with her first child during my first field trip to Tunisia. During our visits together she worried about what to do when the baby was born; she did not want to leave her well-paying job, but she was uncomfortable about leaving her newborn with a maid or other stranger.

While I was back in the United States she had a son, along with a second child, and came up with a truly Tunisian solution to her dilemma: She left the children with her mother, who lived sixty miles away in Bizerte, during the work week. On the weekends she and her husband would visit her parents and spend time with the children. As Claudette, a French friend of Hannan, commented upon my return, "Her mother practically raised both of the children."

This cultural notion of shared parenthood is also illustrated in Faiza's case. Like Hannan, Faiza was a thirty-five-year-old university-educated woman who worked as a bilingual secretary. Her husband, who had a degree in economics, worked for the government, and between the two of them they earned approximately 300 dinars a month. Despite their good income, however, they had decided to move in with her husband's parents, who lived in a traditional Arab house in the *medina*.

"I live with my mother-in-law because we don't have a house," Faiza explained. "When I got married we lived alone and when my two children were born we lived alone. Now it's been seven months that I've been living with my mother-in-law because we don't have a house and we want to buy some land. I want to save a little to buy some land to acquire my own house."

Due to Muslim laws forbidding usury, or the payment of interest, many Tunisian couples desire to purchase their homes outright, which may require some serious financial sacrifices. In Faiza's case, it meant living without her children: "It's fortunate that I have my mother who helps me. I live with my husband's family in Tunis and I only have one room. It's not possible to have the children. Right now my children are with my mother. I'm alone with my husband. It's difficult. I see them once a week. It's hard."

One other form of the long-term visit is those visits from kin or close friends from the hometown who desire to migrate to Tunis. These visits are a common way for job seekers to receive assistance in relocating to the capital, in the classically recognized process of "chain migration." Naima, a fifty-year-old migrant woman from Beja with seven children, describes how her family moved to Tunis: "My husband had a *khal* (maternal uncle) who lived here in Ariana. My uncle brought my husband, and then his aunt (*khala*) afterwards."

"You and your husband and his aunt came . . ."

"We came here. My aunt brought my husband's paternal cousin and he stayed here, too."

The practice of rotating and long-terms visits forces us to reevaluate how we define the household in Tunisia. For rather than being a fairly stable composition, the number of residents tends to fluctuate over time. Likewise, the number of people being supported by a particular household may be significantly greater than simply the people residing there at a particular time. In my interviews, a number of women or their husbands indicated that although their parents or other needy relatives did not live with them, they frequently sent money or other assistance to them, often facing personal and financial hardship to do so, as in Anissa's case.

Anissa, whose network was described in Chapter 4, is a thirty-five-year-old Kairouanese mother of four children who works for the government ministry. Her husband, Hamid, works in government administration also. Together, from their two paychecks, they earn a good income of about 300 dinars a month. After their marriage, Anissa joined Hamid in Tunis, where they have lived in the same downtown apartment for the past fourteen years with Hamid's divorced mother.

Anissa and Hamid not only feed and care for Hamid's mother but also send money to support Anissa's mother and Hamid's father in Kairouan. The support of their relatives is costly, as Hamid laments, "Our income—wife and husband—pays for four children, us two, and my wife's mother and father [who live in Kairouan] and my mother who lives with us. We never get to the end of the month!"

Anissa's story illustrates an important characteristic of women's network ties in Tunis: their continued investment in and care of extended kin across household boundaries. Not only do Anissa and her husband care for her mother-in-law in their home, but a meaningful part of the household income is sent back to the community of origin to support her mother and father-in-law. Thus, although Anissa and her husband live in a modified nuclear household, their budget and behavior reflect a much larger "extended" household that reaches not only over physical household boundaries but also over large geographic areas.

The practice of drop-ins and long-term visits forces us to question the degree to which many seemingly nuclear households are really separate, independent social and economic entities. Daily drop-ins create ties of cooperation and aid between neighboring households. Long-term visits temporarily add kin and network members to the household. And household budgets indicate that household economies may not be limited by the physical boundaries of residence.

Notes

1. During the summer of 1988, the rapidly declining Bourguiban government was facing increasing opposition to its policies, particularly by religious extremist groups. Lorenz and I had the unfortunate timing of visiting the American cultural center located on Avenue Bourguiba in the center of Tunis when one particularly violent clash that involved clubbing and teargassing a procession of protesting university students began in the street below. After a panic-stricken flight through nearby back alleys, we managed to return to our apartment an hour later. Astoundingly, most of our neighbors and friends had already heard about the incident before we even returned home. The evening news and the Tunisian newspapers, however, managed to omit any mention of the event, although the Italian television station showed graphic footage of the conflict, to the glee of many satellite dish owners in Tunis.

7

Women's Religious Celebrations: Status, Class, and Hannan's Friendship Pattern

Ramadan had come in the late spring that year, starting on April 29.[1] It was a hard season for observant Muslims to fast—giving up food, drink (including water, coffee, and tea), smoking, and sex from sunup to sundown—for the days were very long that close to the summer equinox. During the day everyone was irritable: Grumpy taxi and bus drivers drove even more dangerously than usual; people slept at their desks or called in sick; normally lively cafés and stand-up snack bars were deserted; and famished fasters would crowd the food markets arguing vigorously over the prices of specialty foods to buy for the long-awaited dinner breaking the fast (*iftar*).

And yet, it was also a wonderful time of year to celebrate one of the most important Muslim holiday months. Flowers bloomed everywhere, mingling their scents with the baking of many holiday sweets and meals; the days were sunny and clear and warm, but not scorching as they would soon be in July; and the evenings, well the evenings. . . .

Tuesday, May 19. At five o'clock the heat of the day has begun to soften into a warm soft breeze, wafting the delicious odors of simmering holiday meals

*of lamb couscous and shurba (Tunisian soup) and baking makroudh
(date-filled cakes) past Lorenz and me as our noisy moped putters to a stop.
Lorenz parks in front of a tall circle of modern, whitewashed cinder-block
high-rises, not yet ten years old but already starting to look run-down and
faded, perched in a conspicuous group of other similar cités on a hill over-
looking Tunis in the northern well-to-do quarters of the lotissements.*

*We stroll past the collection of a few small stores busily selling last-
minute ingredients such as oil and sugar to harried shoppers, a bank, a
restaurant (now closed), and a café (also deserted at the moment, although
that will change at sundown)—all part of the French concept of a self-
supporting community or cité—and take the creaking elevator up to the
sixth floor. Dressed in a rich purple jaleba (traditional long Tunisian robe)
that does not quite cover her swelling belly, twenty-seven-year-old
Hannan, five months pregnant with her first child, waits for us with her
younger sister, Siehen, who is wearing jeans. This is a new outfit for
Hannan, who is usually dressed in well-tailored professional clothes at her
job as a trilingual secretary for the British embassy.*

*We exchange the traditional kisses on the cheeks; the French cake I have
brought; comments regarding clothes, the heat of the day, the drive on the
moped; and, of course, laughter and smiles.*

*Dinner will not be ready for another two hours, when the sun will finally
set, so Lorenz and I settle down with Hannan's curly-dark-haired husband,
Mounir, in the informal sitting room, furnished with a mix of Tunisian
couches and European armchairs, chatting while the television performs
for us in the background.*

*About fifteen minutes later Mounir excuses us to go to visit his sister
Emira's apartment. He has just bought a new car today—his job as the
head of a bank has been going well—and he wants Emira to see it. Both
Hannan and Mounir are highly educated, with university degrees, and
together they earn 300 dinars a month, a very good income for a young
couple.*

*At any other time of the year we would sit in front of the television with
glasses of hot cooling green tea, eating nuts or dates while waiting for dinner to be served. But it is Ramadan, so in between Hannan and Siehen's
occasional disappearances to check the simmering pots we all gaze hungrily
at a television program on Ramadan foods throughout the Arab world,*

mouth-watering dishes of lamb and rice and honeyed cakes dancing across the screen.

At around seven o'clock Mounir returns, along with Hannan's two un-married sisters, Nejeb and Feirouth, who live together in an apartment in Tunis. Before her marriage last year, Hannan had shared this apartment with her sisters along with another unmarried girlfriend, Dunya, who sud-denly appears just behind Nejeb, Feirouth, and Mounir. Mounir has man-aged to fit two other young women in his new car: Aisha, another of Hannan's unmarried friends that she knows from the university, and his cousin (bint khala), Munjiya. Tunisian car safety laws not being quite as restrictive as those in the United States, he has squeezed one final passenger in: Siehen's (Hannan's sister's) fiancé, Fauzi.

Hannan's apartment is now bustling, filled with her eight guests and the excitement and anticipation that always hangs over every household as dusk creeps over the skyline during Ramadan. The lights of the mosques be-gin to blink on as I look out over the city, and a silence spreads across the deserted streets of the city while everyone waits. Hushed radios and televi-sions mumble as everyone listens expectantly.

And then, finally, "Allaaaaahuuuuu akbaaaaarrrrr," the wail of the muezzin tumbles over the houses at seven-thirty-five P.M. Suddenly there is a rapid rush as all the women run in and out of the kitchen, carrying steaming dishes to the long, elegant wooden table in Hannan's dining room. First a spicy soup (shurba), then brik (a delicious Tunisian egg-filled pastry), then salata mishweea (fried vegetables), and finally a lamb-arti-choke stew. The hunger pangs finally over, we nibble on fruit.

As the women clear off the piles of empty plates from the table, the men return to watch TV in the informal sitting room. Half an hour later, dishes washed and the huge meal settling in our stomachs, Hannan and her sisters and friends sit down at the dining table to help me create and translate my survey questions in correct and logical French and Arabic. I have known Hannan from almost the beginning of my fieldwork, and since Hannan has studied in England and has a university degree, she understands well the purpose of my research and has been a helpful advisor during my year in Tunis.

Questions completed, it is my turn to bring out the European toaster oven that Hannan wants to buy from me. She seems pleased; it is almost new, and much nicer than anything available in Tunisia. We settle on a price, and our business done, Siehen serves up my cake as well as the traditional Ramadan dessert of dra' (a pudding of sorghum).

Now almost nine-thirty, the evening is cool and pleasant and we can hear the streets coming to life below. And so everyone agrees that we should go out for tea to a nearby café where both men and women are welcome. As we sit out at one of the simple metal tables on the sidewalk, the perfume of jasmine and orange blossoms wafting from the street vendors' trays, watching men and women strolling arm in arm eating sugared almonds and peanuts as their children tug on their arms pointing out all the wonderful toys and clothes hanging enticingly in the stores, which have reopened for the holiday evening, I know why so many of my Tunisian friends say that this is their favorite time of year.

HANNAN AND THE FRIENDSHIP PATTERN

When I first met Hannan, she had been married for a year and was expecting her first child. When asked how she had met her husband, Hannan had laughed and replied, "On the bus." Mounir and Hannan dated for a while before getting engaged, a practice that is not common in Tunis except among educated women. Mounir's family, originally from Algeria, was opposed to his choice of a wife. As a result there is much friction between Hannan and her in-laws, as she explains in excellent English: "They're awful. They just don't like me because his mother wanted him to marry somebody else. And he didn't want to. And since that time they were really picky with me." The conflict between Hannan and her in-laws is so great that, even though she visits her husband's family fairly often, Hannan refused to include them in describing her visiting network.

In contrast to her relations with her in-laws, Hannan is very close to her family, especially her sisters, who all live in Tunis: "I am always with my sisters. Just my sisters because now we're living here in Tunis and it's all figured out. So, for example, I used to live with them. We would go shopping together, on Saturday night go to the movies together, with my husband and my sisters to the theater. For me, it's always with my sisters. We get along very well."

Hannan was born in the north of Tunisia and came to Tunis with her sisters several years earlier to study at the university. Although her parents and brother still lived about sixty kilometers away from Tunis, at the time of my first field trip she continued to visit them every one to two weeks. Her frequent visits to her parents on the train (approximately two dinars round-trip per person) were getting to be rather expensive. And as is evident from my Ramadan visit, Hannan and Mounir were delighted when they had finally saved enough to buy a new car.

The closeness of Hannan to her family was demonstrated after the birth of her son, Emir. As described in Chapter 6, since Hannan wanted to continue working but felt that hiring a maid would be uneconomical, she decided to leave Emir with her mother, going to visit him and her parents on weekends and holidays.

In addition to her immediate family, Hannan also visits her grandmother, her three aunts, four uncles, and numerous cousins in her hometown of Jendouba in the north, almost 150 kilometers from Tunis. "Well, for my uncles and aunts, whenever I go to my hometown I go and see them, so I can't tell. Sometimes it happens twice a month. Sometimes it doesn't happen for six months.

"But we're very close. That doesn't mean we're not very close. We call each other on the phone. But I just don't always see them. I see them sometimes when they're traveling and they stop at our house."

The distinguishing feature of Hannan's network is that she has four friends whom she met while studying at the University of Tunis. Two of Hannan's friends live near to her apartment in the *lotissements*. A third friend lives in Sousse, and the fourth friend, Aisha, who came to the Ramadan dinner, shares an apartment with Hannan's sisters in Tunis. Hannan also visits with her sisters' neighbor, whom she befriended when she was sharing the apartment with her sisters.

In contrast to Miriam's and Nura's and Sherifa's visiting networks, many of the households Hannan visits are located far away from Tunis. Hannan's significantly better financial and educational situation enables her to maintain contact with kin and friends over long distances: She has a telephone and a car and is able to read and send letters.

Taking the bus, train, or taxi is also occasionally affordable given Hannan's relatively high income. Hence, Hannan is willing to splurge occasionally on a five dinar round-trip train ticket to Jendouba. There is one other significant characteristic of Hannan's network: She belongs to a social club. "Then there are the people at the British club, because I usually go there. Now I didn't go for at least two weeks because I have been busy. But I usually would go there twice a week, something like that."

Although belonging to a formal social club was not typical of women in my study,[2] several women did belong to an informal social group, often based on their own or their husbands' school or job. Samia, for example, is a forty-five-year-old *Tunisoise* women who lives next door to Zohra Belhedi. Her *Tunisoise* husband, who is both her *wuld 'am* and her *wuld khal* (due to multiple intermarriages), studied at the Sorbonne and currently holds a well-paying position in the government ministry. Samia gets together every week or so with a group of women from different parts of the city (the affluent *menzehs*, and the exclusive suburbs of Dindin and Carthage), who are the wives of her husband's former private high school *(lycée)* friends and colleagues at work. As Samia was quick to point out, these friends are well placed; one woman's husband is in the upper administration of UNESCO, and another is currently in Jordan, where her husband is an ambassador.

"We used to see each other once a week," she explains in perfect French. "Now it's once a month or every twenty days. We all get together, the three, four, five friends."

"All the group gets together once a week, each time at someone's home," adds her daughter Lilia, also in excellent French. "They are all members of a little party, you see."

The distinguishing feature of women with friendship networks is the inclusion of three or more friends whom the woman knows from school, work, or her husband's work. Although these friendships certainly provide emotional support and companionship, they also give women access to difficult-to-obtain resources or assistance not available from the neighborhood or kin group. In the case of my friendship with Hannan, I supplied her with various "exotic" American foods from the U.S. commissary such as cake mixes, as well as selling her our toaster oven.

Friendship networks are quite large, ranging from a minimum of eight households to a maximum of thirty-four households,[3] with a mean size of twenty-two households for the women I surveyed. Given the amorphous size of women's social clubs or groups, women with this style would often become frustrated when I would ask them to list all their friends, tending to give round numbers, such as "about fifteen" friends. Although these networks include an average of seven or more friends, kin still make up the majority of the network, with a mean number of fourteen kin-related households.

Like Hannan, women with "friendship networks" have significantly higher educational levels than women in my survey with kin exclusive or neighbor networks (see Table A2.2, Appendix 2). Furthermore, four of the eight women with friendship networks were currently employed in upper-level white-collar positions: Three were secretaries and one was a teacher. Latifa was the only woman to have a home business, and upon my return to Tunis in 1993 her sewing business had become so successful that she had actually opened up her own shop on a nearby street. The high proportion of women with friendship networks in the formal workforce is also significantly different from women with the other two network patterns.

All of the women's husbands had either studied at the *lycée* (high school) or university, and, with the exception of Kareem, Latifa's husband, who owned a driving school (and his own car), they all held professional and secure positions: in the government, at a bank, as an engineer, and in managerial positions for the police and military. All of the couples were quite well-to-do, with the highest incomes, on the average, in my survey (345.6 dinars per month).

Tellingly, reflecting their higher educational levels and perhaps more "Westernized" orientation, of the eight women with friendship networks whom I interviewed for my survey, only two responded in Arabic. Hannan answered my questions in English and the remaining five women answered in French.

Significantly, as Hannan's own story demonstrates, however, while women's education and employment appear to be clearly related to the kinds of networks they form, migration does not. An equal proportion of migrant and *Tunisoise* women form friendship networks. And there is no significant relationship between the kind of networks women participate in and whether the woman is a migrant.

Contemporary couple viewing the festivities at their fetiha (engagement party). The child waving a candle in front of them symbolizes good fortune.

One explanation for the strongly significant relationship between women's work, education, and the kinds of people in their networks is that women who spend many years in school and at work are more likely to meet and become friends with "outsiders." Yet this cannot be a complete explanation because many of the women with neighbor and kin exclusive networks also worked prior to their marriages, and a number continue to work either out of their homes or in the formal economy after marriage.

A second and perhaps more compelling argument is that due to these women's better education and resulting prestigious employment (and their marriages to similarly well-educated and skilled men), they have higher incomes and hence more resources to spend on exchanging visits with a larger and more diffuse network. Women's income is very strongly related to the number of people in their network, as illustrated in Table A2.4 (see Appendix 2). The higher the woman's monthly budget, the more kin, friends, and neighbors she is likely to visit. Quite simply, wealthier women can afford to network: to make and serve expensive sweets and elaborate Ramadan dinners for their guests, to pay for taxis and car rides across the city and country to network members, and to keep up with the expensive gift exchanges required of network members at holidays and life cycle celebrations.

Tellingly, however, neither household income nor women's educational level is significantly related to migration for my survey in general. Although certain categories of migrant women are poor and uneducated, like Miriam and Nura (typically forming neighbor or kin exclusive networks), a comparable number, like Hannan, have emigrated to the capital city *because of* their high education, seeking skilled jobs for themselves and/or their husbands. As a result, it would appear that it is not migration that influences the number of households and kin in women's networks but the inability of *lower-income* migrant women to afford trips to friends and kin back in the hometown.

Hannan's case also illustrates another important characteristic of women with friendship networks: their greater autonomy from the kin group. Hannan, for example, selected her own husband, did not marry anyone from her own region, and lives in a nuclear household without any relatives. Women with friendship networks tend to choose their own spouses, marry nonkin, be less concerned with region of origin in their selection of a spouse, and live in nuclear households rather than with kin (see Table A2.3, Appendix 2). This does not mean that kin are unimportant, as Hannan's intimate ties and frequent visits to her family underscore. Indeed, women with friendship networks typically had the highest number of kin in their networks, listing an average of 14.4 kin-related households.

Rather, women with friendship networks appear to be less dependent on and controlled by the corporate kin group (and neighbors, who in many ways are substitute kin). Given their affluent positions and fairly secure incomes and pensions through employment in the government and industry, these women are far less concerned with the struggles for survival that Miriam and Nura face daily. Instead of investing heavily in a closed group of kin or neighbors, women with friendship networks, like Hannan, look to their networks as vehicles of social mobility, seeking to maximize their visits and exchanges with a wide, diffuse network of potentially useful connections.

Yet although these women may be breaking with tradition in their choice of husbands and more independent residence patterns, their efforts to move up within the social system continue to follow the age-old tradition of exchange and reciprocity through visits. It is during these well-to-do women's visits at religious holidays (*'Eedet*) and life cycle events (*mounesibet*) that the boundaries of class and changing ties of affiliation and disaffiliation are most evidently displayed.

VISITS AT RELIGIOUS HOLIDAYS (*'EEDET*)

Not surprisingly, in contrast to men, whose religious life centers on formal religious institutions such as the mosque or religious schools (*madrasa*) and teachers (*imam*), for women in Tunis, religious observance frequently centers around the bustling social domestic world of visits, particularly during *'Eedet* (religious holidays). For many women, *'Eedet* are viewed not as a time to pray or to focus on religious study (although some of the more conservative Islamist women are calling for this) but as a critical time to exchange visits with their entire larger extended network, demonstrating and affirming the complete extent of their social ties. This is no small burden, since many women's networks (especially those of wealthy women) include up to a hundred or more people, as Samia, Zohra's *Tunisoise* neighbor, pointed out: "Our cousins, our brothers, uncles, cousins of a cousin; a hundred people come to visit me the day of *'Eed Sgheer* and the second day. Those who don't come during the year, it's the day of *'Eed* that they come to see you."

Although daily drop-in visits rarely involve more than the offering of green or red tea, visits during religious holidays are much more formal and elaborate affairs. One of the unique features of women's observance of religious holidays in Tunis is the preparation of expensive, elaborate meals, dishes, and sweets that are exchanged during special visits, such as our Ramadan dinner with Hannan.

Women's work as hostesses is no small matter. Cooking and food preparation is immensely time-consuming, since everything must be prepared from scratch and only extremely well-to-do households can afford appliances such as microwave ovens, blenders, or even refrigerators and stoves (which may explain why foreign cooking equipment, such as the toaster oven I sold Hannan, was in such great demand). Furthermore, many of the special dishes typically offered to visitors during holidays, such as *baklawa* (a pastry made of filo dough and nuts and honey), *usben* (stuffed sheep's intestines), and *couscous* (steamed semolina that can be served with many special sauces), require very expensive ingredients such as nuts, honey, dried fruit, and meat or fish, a kilo of which often costs the equivalent of a working-class person's daily wages.

Women take the work of hospitality quite seriously. An important topic of conversation in almost any social gathering of women is the exchange of recipes and information about where to buy special ingredients. Women also enjoy describing in detail the amount, kind, and quality of food served at weddings or other celebrations they have attended. This information is not frivolous women's chit chat but important comparative news that could have a significant impact on the status of the woman and her household. A woman's failure to provide as equally lavish a spread as her relatives or other network members will not only reflect badly on her own skills as a hostess and the hospitality of the family but may bring into question her ability to "keep up" socially with the Tunisian version of the "Joneses."

The visits during Ramadan, *Moulid*, '*Eed ekkabeer*, and '*Eed essgheer* are especially significant because they are not only an affirmation of women's ties but a visible demonstration of the family's wealth and status.

Ramadan

Technically and ideally, for Muslims, Ramadan is not a holiday but a month of self-denial and prayer to bring one closer to God. However, for many Tunisians, as Amal, an educated university professor, complains, the self-denial of the day is simply a prelude to a busy social schedule of eating and drinking and entertaining at night: "It's catastrophic! They don't work; they work a little. People sit around, they shop, they eat, they shop, shop, eat. And God doesn't like Ramadan like that. He doesn't like people eating a lot during Ramadan. You're supposed to eat only one thing—something simple. Not that during the day you do everything according to religion and then eat the entire day's food all in the night. It's not good at all. Quite the opposite." Amal's opinion, however, is quite radical. Most Tunisians, like Hannan, prepare a sumptuous meal of numerous courses for the "breaking fast" dinner (*iftar*). So much food is eaten at night during Ramadan that despite fasting for thirty days, many women complained of gaining weight during the month!

The importance of serving one's guests well and generously is illustrated in the dinner we were served by Hannan. Although it was a work night (Thursday) and Hannan was five months pregnant, with the assistance of her sister Siehen she still managed to create a six-course meal for her guests.

Ramadan, however, is certainly not the only holiday when women are expected to exchange visits and elaborate dishes. During *Moulid*, the holiday celebrating the Prophet Muhammed's birth, and *'Eed essgheer*, the two-day celebration at the end of the month of Ramadan, women make special sweets, which they exchange during visits with relatives and network members.

'Eed essgheer and Moulid

We arrived at the Belhedi's house around eleven o'clock. Sami, their eldest son, met us at the door, explaining that the rest of the family was out making a visit to another home. So we sat down to wait, nibbling on a plate of baklawa and other special 'Eed cakes and drinking some coffee that Sami had quickly reheated for us.[4]

Not much later, Jemila, Zohra, and Mohammed returned, all wearing fancy new clothes. Jemila and Zohra looked quite stunning decorated in their gold jewelry. With a laugh and smile, Zohra took my box of ghaeeba, a kind of Tunisian shortbread that, just last week, we had baked together in her kitchen.

A quiet knock on the door announced the arrival of Rania, Jemila's next-door neighbor, whose engagement we would celebrate in the coming month. She briefly visited alone with Jemila in the formal living room, while Zohra and I started preparing lunch, and the men sat in the informal living room eating cakes and watching soccer on the television.

Around one-thirty some friends of Zohra (a woman she had known from school, plus her husband) came to visit. They traded stories about each other's families and the people they knew for about half an hour or so, while Zohra served us all tea with pine nuts and baklawa and other holiday cakes. Then as the couple were leaving, Mohammed gave the woman's husband a Cuban cigar.

Zohra and Mohammed then went to change clothes into something more casual and inexpensive. They were going to Hammam Lif to visit Mohammed's brother and wanted us to come with them, but we declined since Lorenz was studying for his final exams. Before we left, Zohra handed me a plate with a variety of little cakes, which we carefully packed onto our moped to take home.

During '*Eed essgheer* and *Moulid* expensive, elaborate sweets are prepared and exchanged with kin and network members. For *Moulid*, women serve a traditional pudding made from grinding highly expensive pine nuts (*pignoli*) into a paste, which is then served to guests. At '*Eed essgheer,* women serve an immense variety of nut- and dried-fruit-filled cakes.

The expense of the sweets, as well as the tea served, varies directly with the household's wealth. "For '*Eed essgheer* we make sweets," began Hind, a poor maid whose husband had been unemployed for years. "People who have money make *baklawa*. It's expensive: thirty dinars for a few kilos. And those who don't have money make *makroudh* [a dough with date filling] or *ghaeeba* [cakes from sorghum flour] or biscuits. That's all. Each person gives everyone a plate. She gives one and the other person gives one back."

Likewise, Douzha, the poor widow whose neighbor network was described in Chapter 6, answered my questions about what she does at '*Eed:* "For '*Eed essgheer* we make *ghaeeba*."

"Those people who have money make *baklawa* or *kak elwarqa* [cookies with almonds]," added her neighbor. "And we poor people make *makroudh* or *ghaeeba*—it's cheaper."

Most significant here is the way that these completely unrelated women could consistently articulate a clear relationship between one's

wealth and the cakes served, indicating the presence of a fairly formal-
ized food-status structure.

The choice of tea served follows very specific rules according to the occasion and hostess's wealth. Plain green or red tea, heavily infused with
sugar and simmered for twenty minutes or longer, is the least-expensive
offering. Generally the addition of nuts to tea indicates a more formal affair or wealthier household. Peanuts are the least expensive nut to add;
almonds are used as a moderately expensive offering. Pine nuts are used
only on very special occasions by wealthy families, given their extremely
high cost.

At 'Eed essgheer, in addition to the exchange of cakes and the requisite
serving of tea, gifts of clothes or money are also given to children in the
immediate family, as Sherifa describes: "At 'Eed, I go to visit my parents'
home. I go to visit them and we visit together. And we make baklawa
and we make ghaeeba and we make kak elwarqa and we drink soda and
we come and go [i.e., exchange visits]. We go out the day of 'Eed. And we
buy new clothes for 'Eed—for my son: shoes, socks, and pants. Or skirts
and blouses. A tie. And I give to the children who come to me—to the
little ones—I give money. I give a dinar, five hundred millimes."

Part of the purpose of making and exchanging sweets during religious holidays is to demonstrate the woman's cooking skill and the
wealth of her family. Since everyone trades plates of sweets, the exchange is primarily symbolic: At the end of the day there is no net increase or decrease in cakes per household (except, of course, for those
sweets you have eaten).

'Eed ekkabeer

Like the other holidays, 'Eed ekkabeer centers around the preparation
and exchange of food, in this case, specialties made from a sacrificed
sheep. This Muslim holiday, which reenacts the Old Testament story of
Abraham's sacrifice of his son Isaac, requires that all Muslims who are
able should sacrifice a sheep in remembrance of their supreme commit-
ment and obedience to God.

The month before 'Eed ekkabeer, the marketplaces and open spaces of
Tunis are filled with the baaing and braying of herds of sheep, driven in

*A sheep being sacrificed at
'Eed ekkabeer.*

by hopeful farmers from the countryside. The baas and odors of sheep then slowly move into the courtyards and garages of both wealthy villas and modest homes, as each household feeds and fattens the sheep in preparation for the upcoming holiday.

As on the holidays of *'Eed essgheer, Moulid,* and *Ramadan,* the dishes prepared for *'Eed ekkabeer* require much time and expense. Purchase of the sheep alone is extremely costly. (A good-sized sheep costs 80 to 100 dinars.) Correspondingly, the size, gender, and number of sheep sacrificed reflect the wealth of the household, as Hind, a mother of seven who worked as a maid, observes: "At *'Eed ekkabeer* there is a sheep: It's expensive. I buy a small male sheep. I buy it for forty or fifty dinars. Then you sacrifice it." In contrast, a neighbor of the Belhedi family, whose two married sons were visiting for the holiday, sacrificed a total of three large sheep, one for each nuclear household. Such extreme expense, however, is a sign of a very well-to-do family.

The morning of the sacrifice is a busy affair. While the men work at cutting and cleaning the sheep, the women are busy in the kitchen, saving and storing part of the meat and preparing holiday delicacies such as *usben,* a Tunisian specialty made by stuffing the sheep's intestines with various innards saved from the sheep. The sheep's skin must also be cleaned and salted and dried. Since the butchering and cleaning and cooking take all day, typically women spend the first day of *'Eed ekkabeer* at home or at the house of their parents or in-laws preparing specialties from the sheep. Then on the second day the women, their husbands, and their children make formal visits to their extended family, often bringing gifts of food, as was illustrated by Tahar's *Moulid* visit to his fiancée Behija's family in Chapter 4.

'Eed ekkabeer, like the other important holidays, is often an occasion for migrants to return to their hometown, particularly if the visit can be combined with another special occasion such as a wedding or circumcision. Anissa, the Kairouanese working mother whose income helps to support her parents in her hometown, for example, took two weeks off from her job in the government to return to Kairouan. "I went at *'Eed ekkabeer.* I was on vacation. I went for fourteen days to see my mother— the whole family. We held a circumcision for my son."

Anissa's decision to celebrate her son's circumcision in Kairouan reflects not only her continued investment in her home community, despite migration, but also the importance of including extended kin and other network members in life cycle events.

VISITS AT LIFE CYCLE EVENTS OR *MOUNESIBET*

Life cycle events, like holidays, are a time to affirm network ties. Women are expected to make formal visits to their kin, neighbors, and friends not only at the obvious life cycle transitions such as births, deaths, circumcisions, and weddings but also if someone is seriously ill or has returned from the *hajj* (pilgrimage to Mecca) or a trip overseas, or has a birthday, or perhaps has just succeeded in completing the *sixième* (sixth grade) or *bac* (high school completion exam), or even, as in the case of Hannan's Ramadan dinner, to congratulate someone (say *mabrouk*) on the purchase of a major item such as a car or house. These many and frequent events, which fall under the general term *mounesibet,* or "social

On the beach: washing sheepskins from the sacrificed sheep at 'Eed ekkabeer.

occasions," all afford women the opportunity to reaffirm more distant, yet still important, social ties.

In my interviews women would explain their ties to these more distant network members in terms of the events when they would go to visit them. Selwa, the migrant woman whose husband was a shoemaker and whose maternal uncles were "putting on *bourgeois* airs," explained her much closer ties to her paternal uncle: "I have an *'amm* in Lafayette. I love him very much. We go. When he is sick or something, we go. Or like when he went on the *hajj* to Mecca. When he returned we went to greet him. We see him at *mounesibet*."

Women not only visit at these social occasions but usually also bring gifts, to help the family at a time of need. "If someone gives birth to a boy or girl, perhaps they don't have money at this time. So everyone does something, you understand? Or everyone brings something," explains Amal, the divorced university professor, in Arabic. "The family doesn't have clothes for the baby; they don't have this, they don't have that. Perhaps they don't have anything so that they can eat well. So someone brings meat, someone brings eggs. We bring things like that.

Perhaps there are a lot of guests there. So that the mother has something to offer the guests to eat, someone puts meat in the fridge in order to cook for all the people."

As Amal points out, gifts are given not to the individual but to help out the household at a time of need. Significantly, one of the most important contributions by guests is the provision of food, which is not consumed by the family but offered to other guests, hence enabling them to afford the costs of serving and hosting so many visitors.

Like births, on the occasion of a death or illness, kin and other network members are also expected to help out. During the first days after the death, the immediate family is not permitted to cook, clean, or otherwise undertake household responsibilities. Instead, extended kin and sometimes neighbors or friends assume these tasks. Throughout the official mourning period bereaved family members remain at home, praying for the dead person and receiving visits from friends and relatives, who bring gifts of food or money.

"We Tunisians, when someone dies we can't work or go out or anything," Boujemaa, Nawal's ten-year-old son, began.

"Yes," his thirty-eight-year-old mother, and wife of a well-to-do farmer, added in Arabic, "after the death of my father for three days I didn't cook. Three days! The family cooked for us. We worshipped a long time. We sat [remained at home] sixteen days. And then later it's our turn, we give back to those who helped. We alternate." Likewise, Hind, a fifty-year-old maid whose son had been killed in a hit-and-run car accident a few months before, recounts: "After the death of my son, people didn't give money. They gave macaroni, they gave oil, tomatoes, sugar. Everyone, I don't know, everyone came to the house, came to the house. We Arabs, like when there is a death in a house, all the people bring something. There are people who give money. There are people who give stuff to care for the home: macaroni, tomatoes, sugar, oil. Stuff like that. Everyone came to the house."

"I'm like that, too. Also if there is someone who is sick, it's the same. I know who gives—like if I saw someone bring something or someone didn't bring something, then tomorrow, I'll do the same. At the time of a death, I bring them, like, macaroni, sugar, tomatoes, a carton of milk."

As both Hind and Nawal emphasize, gifts and assistance offered at the time of a death are given with the assumption that later, in a similar crisis, the favor will be returned. As a result, a continuous flow of food and assistance moves through the network to various households at times of need.

The obligations occasioned by receiving so many gifts is a debt that is quite costly to return. "I gave a lot of gifts this year," thirty-year-old Aya asserts in French as she sits by me on the beach dressed in a long gown and covered by the conservative veil or *hijab.* "For the *sixième,* for the *concours* (another educational exam). And I had others who passed the *bac* (high school exam) and also circumcisions."

"I spent almost 150 dinars this year for all these gifts," exclaims Aya, who despite the injunction of her conservative, high school–educated husband to veil his equally educated wife, obviously has quite a busy visiting and exchange network. "Because I had my son's circumcision during Ramadan. Everyone brought gifts. And I have to return them!"

Births, deaths, and circumcisions are costly events, but there is no question that the most expensive life cycle celebrations revolve around marriage. Gifts and contributions at weddings, like most other social events, not only assist the family but demonstrate the status of the donor.

"If there is a marriage celebration all of the women go to the house where the celebration is held and they bring money," Amal elaborates. "Usually they bring a dinar. If they are from the middle class, you know, they bring five dinars. And if they're really well-to-do, they bring ten dinars."

Although the individual contributions at a wedding may seem small, if all the extended kin and network members contribute, the costs of the numerous wedding celebrations can easily be accumulated. Hence, by pooling their resources at weddings or other celebrations the extended networks of the bride and groom assist individual households in financing the exorbitant costs of marriage, as Amal cogently illustrates: "The family in Tunisia is not small. The family in Tunisia is the father and the mother and the children and the grandparents and the mother's sister and the father's sister and the nieces and nephews, you understand? . . . A large family has many people, even a thousand. And whoever comes to a wedding brings something to the wedding. If everyone brings ten dinars, you see, ten dinars times a thousand people. That's a lot."

Poignantly, Amal concludes by explaining in a few insightful words the economic significance of networks that I have been describing in this book: "Why do we give gifts? Because people, each time they do something they need to spend money. And afterwards, everyone returns the money, either equally or a little more; but it's not possible to return less. For example, I bring five dinars to a wedding. After the wedding, people have to bring to an event of mine five dinars, or ten dinars, or seven dinars. That means, what have they done? Made a bank, you see. You bring money to the bank. Then at your wedding, at a circumcision or something, everyone returns the money to you. This way you have a happy wedding, you can do lots of things and everyone helps each other out."

Notes

1. The Muslim calendar is based on lunar months. Hence, the month of Ramadan shifts backward every solar year.
2. Although several of my more well-to-do friends described the existence of social clubs for women in Tunis, Hannan and Najet (the unmarried university student described in Chapters 4 and 6) were the only women I met who actually participated in such clubs.
3. Due to the ambiguity of the number of friends in the networks of women who socialize with a group of friends, these figures are a conservative estimate of the actual number of friends listed.
4. Men usually do not do the "work" of preparing and serving food to visitors. However, they will sometimes step in and find something to offer unexpected guests if no women are available.

8

Conclusions

Sherifa, Miriam, Nura, and Hannan: working women and house-wives, migrants and original inhabitants of Tunis, university gradu-ates and women who can barely read and write. They live with their rel-atives and far away from their relatives; they have arranged marriages and meet their potential husbands on the bus; they buy new cars and can barely afford the eighty-millime bus ride to see their sisters on holi-days. Each woman is married, a Muslim, a Tunisian, and in her own way unique, an individual with her own life story, her own personal daily challenges and successes.

And yet, in many ways, each woman shares a common thread that is woven through all of their lives: their shared struggles to survive in an unpredictable and rapidly urbanizing and developing nation. Whether they argue with their in-laws like Hannan or spend every moment of their waking lives with their sisters-in-law like Sherifa, there is no ques-tion that their ties to their families are the central part of their daily lives. Whether they share food and baby sitting with their neighbors, like Nura, or with their relatives, like Miriam and Sherifa—or perhaps it is car rides and toasters with friends, like Hannan—each woman relies on her network to provide the financial, material, and social support neces-sary to cope with the daily economic and social insecurities that she faces. And whether they hold elaborate, six-course Ramadan dinners like Hannan or, like Miriam and Nura, bake simple cheap Ramadan cakes such as *ghaeeba* for their holiday guests, each woman is distinctly aware of the importance of hospitality and exchange with the people in her network, conscious that poor hospitality or a failure to visit at critical times can rupture the ties and close her out of the social world that she so carefully nurtures.

Although each woman's network is distinct, their ties fall into three complementary patterns: the kin exclusive network, neighbor networks, and the friendship pattern. Each of these network styles can be viewed not as separate and contrasting, but rather as a variation in the strategies women employ to survive in differing socioeconomic environments. All three network patterns are formed first and foremost around a critical core of kin; neighbors and friends become supplementary additions to the network rather than replacements for kin.

As my case studies and survey data reveal, the central determinants of women's social ties and network strategies in Tunis are income and class, and, to a lesser degree, the related factor of education and women's employment opportunities. Migration as an independent variable has an unclear impact, perhaps because migrants are not a homogeneous category; both educated and illiterate, wealthy and poor, and working women and housewives migrate.

The primary factor affecting the size of women's networks is clearly household income. Only wealthy women can afford the lavish hospitality and frequent visits required of the upper and upper middle classes. Poorer women, who do not have the money, time, means of transportation, or household help required for frequent entertaining, tend to restrict their visits to nearby kin and neighbors.

Significantly, this finding poses a strong challenge to modernization theories, which implicitly expect that an increase in material wealth and consumption of Western goods goes hand in hand with a falling away from "traditional" activities and values. For the women in my study, more income simply allowed women to spend more money and time on the time-honored Arab custom of hospitality and visiting. Rather than taking vacations to Europe, wealthier women such as Fauzia preferred to spend several months visiting relatives in the hometown; instead of spending money on nights out at restaurants or the movies, well-to-do women such as Hannan spent fortunes on expensive sweets and ingredients for entertaining or hired maids to cook elaborate meals for guests; and purchases of "status goods" such as cars and refrigerators were not intended to increase a family's leisure time through Sunday drives or a stock of fast-food in the fridge but to make visits to faraway network members easier and allow women to prepare more exotic dishes with perishable ingredients.

For the women in my study, visiting networks clearly define class and social boundaries. Since visits and hospitality must be reciprocal, their exchange is generally restricted to households of similar economic and social backgrounds. Women's access to goods and services is thus determined by their economic and social ability to exchange similar goods; whereas well-to-do Hannan uses her network to obtain hard-to-get, expensive, imported status goods, poor, uneducated Miriam's network, which has little wealth or material goods, offers instead free labor such as a sister-in-law to baby sit so Miriam can work. Sherifa, on the other hand, depends on her old aristocratic *Tunisoise* ties, with relatives placed in high-status positions such as embassies in Italy, to obtain visas for shopping trips to Europe with her sister-in-law.

Significantly, since social class in Tunisia depends not only on wealth but also on region of origin, most women's visits are between kin or people from the same region, creating within the city small, homogenous pockets based on region of origin. These closed, bounded networks are further reinforced by the preference for marriages with kin or families from the same region.

In this study, women's education and employment appeared to be related to some degree to greater independence from the kin group: All of the women who had the more open friendship network pattern were significantly more highly educated and held the highest-status jobs. At the outset these findings might suggest that women's higher education and their access to income independent of their husbands result in their greater domestic power and hence more freedom in selecting not only their spouses or residences but also their friends. However, the stories of Aya, who despite a high school education and a job in insurance was mandated to wear the *hijab* by her husband and to stop working and socializing with her European friends; the case of Anissa, the Kairouanese high school graduate who is currently an administrator at the University of Tunis, whose marriage was arranged and whose network consists of only kin; and the highly kin-dominated world of Sherifa, a Tunisoise woman who left high school to marry the man she loved, provide a puzzling challenge to this analysis.

A second alternative explanation may be suggested by the high number of women with friendship networks who responded to my survey in French or even English. Since language choice in Tunisia reflects one's social orientation or aspirations, it is possible that women who prefer to speak a foreign language also prefer to identify and socialize with foreigners. Hence perhaps women with friendship networks have accepted Euro-American ideals of gender and social relationships, including employment outside of the home, as well as an increased comfort with interacting with outsiders.

Further studies are necessary to answer some of these questions, but one conclusion can clearly be drawn from my data: Regardless of education, employment, or migration, kin still form the central and majority of all women's networks. The overwhelming evidence in this study for the persistence of kin ties stands in strong contrast to earlier descriptions of the disintegration of the "traditional" Arab family in North Africa. More recent studies in Tunisia, Morocco, Algeria, Egypt, Yemen, Jordan, Bangladesh, and Kuwait tend to confirm my findings, illustrating the persistence of assistance and support between kin, the continuation of marriages with kin, and the cohabitation with and economic support of kin.[1] These ties appear to persist despite national and international migration (Stevenson 1997).

One explanation for the conflicting evidence on family change is that studies that have described the disintegration of the Tunisian family have focused primarily on internal household relations, examining such questions as parent-child relations and husband-wife conflicts as reflected in abuse or divorce. This more psychological approach examines the dynamics of interactions *within* the household, implicitly considered to be bounded and separate from the "outside world." Studies that have emphasized the resilience of the Arab family, in contrast, tend to take an anthropological approach, focusing on the household within the cultural and social context: examining the ties *between* households and looking at the flow of resources and people across household boundaries.

As my research demonstrates, in Tunis household composition is extremely fluid. Widowed and orphaned children, for example, often move about among their relatives, visiting each household for a few months so that the burden of their care is distributed among kin; likewise, migrants may temporarily take up residence with kin while settling into a new urban environment; and relatives may return to the hometown from Europe or the capital city for long vacations to stay with kin. Not only do people move between households, but critical resources such as food, child care, and money often are transferred over theoretical household boundaries: Adult children frequently support elderly parents who live far away, migrants send remittances back home, and nearby kin or neighbors provide food to those in need and watch each other's children.

Not only is it clear that people and resources are transferred over household boundaries, but my findings that kin often deliberately reside next door to each other—on the same street, in the same apartment building, or in subdivided villas—force us to redefine what we consider to be a household. As I have argued, it would appear that the extended household in Tunis has in a number of cases simply moved "up" or "out"—becoming the "extended street" or "extended apartment building"—in response to cramped urban housing conditions and changing economic options.

Many women in Tunis, such as Sherifa, who lives next door to her husband's four brothers and their wives, continue to spend their daily lives in the company of the neighboring extended family. For these women and their husbands it would appear that new ideals of consumption—the desire to have one's own kitchen, bathroom, living room furniture, etc.—have prompted the younger generation in Tunisia not necessarily to move away from the extended family but rather to increase the number of buildings and material goods such as refrigerators and showers that each nuclear subgroup now owns. While this shift reflects, perhaps, a desire for couples to have more autonomy over their own income and expenses, the expectation that neighboring kin will provide economic and social support suggests that the finances of the extended "kin street" or "kin apartment building" still continue to be interdependent.

Not only does this study challenge our definitions of the household, but it also produces some most unexpected findings regarding the patrilinearity of the Tunisian family. In contrast to the long-established ideal of the patrilineal and patrilocal Arab family, women in my study actually showed a preference for visiting consanguineal kin, and they were equally as likely to live with or near their own kin as their husband's kin. One could explain the results as another consequence of development, citing women's increasing rights and reforms in the family status law as causes of a trend toward the Euro-American bilateral kinship pattern. Yet several ethnographic studies of women in the region[2] also indicate a bilateral pattern for Arab women's kin relations, in contrast to the ideal preference for patrilineal kin.

These data suggest that perhaps there is a *gendered* experience of kinship. Although adult men in the Middle East may indeed live in a patrilineal world—the picture that has dominated most of our literature—perhaps Arab women's social world and ties have always been more bilateral in nature. Evidence from studies of women's networks in Lebanon, Iran, and Jordan[3] indicates that in other parts of the Middle East women and men have distinctly different networks, which may reach into completely separate political and social sectors. If women and men live in separate social worlds, as Abu Lughod (1985) argues, then it is reasonable to assume that their choices of which kin ties to activate and maintain may also not necessarily be identical. Historical studies that could determine the nature of women's (rather than men's) kin ties in the past, as well as studies comparing the networks of men and women in other parts of the Middle East, would be of great assistance in answering some of these questions.

Nineteen-year-old Jemila's thick, dark curls hang over the photo album of her friends and family, as we giggle and smile at the stories she is telling about them. Suddenly serious, she pauses to explain to me, her American friend, why these photos are so important. Why, even though she is a university student and Sami, her twenty-four-year-old brother, holds an excellent job as an engineer, they still live with their parents. And why seven years later, despite her university education, despite her friendships with foreigners, and her marriage to a man she will meet while vacationing at the beach, Jemila will still come to the city every week to visit her parents and brothers, choosing not to hold a job in the formal economy but rather running a successful and flexible home-based enterprise making pottery for her husband's business:

"One doesn't leave home in Tunisia—the family home—because, well, you can't. It's not done," Jemila asserts emphatically. "To leave, just isn't done, especially for the girls. But even for a boy, it's very rare. We see how the Europeans live and we know that they are very free. So we revolt. And then afterwards we accept."

"For example, I will speak of my mother. My mother was one of the first in the older generation that also thought that a couple should start out on their own and not be limited by what was traditional. But because of living in Tunisian society, now she begins to have regrets. For example, for me, she doesn't talk of beginning a life alone—no. She would like me to marry traditionally. Yes, it's true that things are changing. You can live like the Europeans, but not if you want to be part of Tunisian society."

Notes

1. Royaume du Maroc (1996); Guerraoui (1996); Adel (1996); Mahfoudh-Draoui (1993); Holmes-Eber (1997a, 1997b); Davis and Davis (1989); Bouraoui (1986); Rugh (1984); Singerman (1995); McCann (1997); Stevenson (1997); Amin (1998); Ghabra (1987); Abu Lughod (1993, 1986); Barakat (1988, 1993).
2. Bilateral kinship patterns have been described in Morocco (Davis and Davis 1989), Egypt (Hoodfar 1997), the Sudan (Michael 1997), and for Palestinians in Kuwait (Ghabra 1987).
3. See Hegland (1991), Joseph (1983), and Ginat (1982).

Appendix I:
The Survey

From June to August 1987, I interviewed thirty-six women about their social networks and kin relations using an open-ended survey format. Although the questions were standardized, participants could respond to each question in as much detail for as long as they cared to. Survey interviews typically lasted about one and one-half hours, although frequently I would remain chatting with the women informally for another half hour or more after the tape recorder had been turned off. Many of the survey interviews became a group undertaking because everyone under the woman's umbrella or tent wanted to participate. The survey interviews were written in both French and Tunisian Arabic; women could respond in whichever language they preferred. Thirty-four of the interviews were taped and transcribed.

Survey participants were contacted in two ways. First, eleven of the thirty-six women were introduced to me through the assistance of friends in Tunis, a networks or "snowball" survey approach. The remaining twenty-five women were selected randomly on the beaches of La Goulette and La Marsa. Of the twenty-seven women whom I approached on the beach to participate in the survey, only two women (or less than 8 percent) refused.

To determine whether the survey accurately captured women's network relations, several women whose networks I had observed were surveyed initially as a pretest. These women were delighted to make comments on how I could improve the survey, comments that I later incorporated into the questions. The demographic characteristics of these women were similar to the survey sample in general, indicating that my observational and survey data probably focused on a similar cross-section of women.

Because position in the life cycle may significantly affect network composition (Leigh 1982), my survey focused on married women with unmarried children remaining at home. The women in my survey had an average age of thirty-five, with a range from twenty-three to fifty-seven years of age. Interestingly enough, although I screened participants by asking them if they were married, three widowed (although no divorced) women were included because they had responded yes, they were married. One single woman and one grandmother were included in the survey for comparative purposes.

The majority of the women (65 percent) and their husbands (79 percent) in the survey were first- or second-generation migrants to Tunis, reflecting the large rate of in-migration to the city over the past half century. The income, educational levels, and work experience of the women varied greatly. Household budgets ranged from a minimum of 60 dinars to a maximum of 600 dinars per month, with a mean of 216.5 (an average that corresponded almost exactly to the annual average household income of 2,66.5 dinars per year at the time; Institut National de la Statistique 1999).

The majority (77.7 percent) of women were housewives, although 60 percent had worked prior to their marriage. Seven women (19.4 percent) earned income on the side from home work such as sewing or hairdressing. Of the eight women who were currently employed outside of the home, one was a maid, three worked in education, and four held secretarial or office positions.

According to census and employment surveys administered during the time of my own survey research, Tunisian women's employment rates appeared to range from 21.8 percent in 1984 (Tunisia I.N.S. 1984, ser. 1, v. 5); to 20.3 percent in 1989 (Institut National de la Statistique 1999); to 22.9 percent in 1994 (Institut National de la Statistique 1999). With regard to employment, then, my sample is fairly representative; 22 percent of the women in my survey held jobs outside the home.

Women in the survey had all levels of education, ranging from no schooling to a university degree, with a mean number of 6.8 years of education. In comparison to national census statistics on women in Tunis, the women in my survey were better educated than average. This higher level of education may, in part, be due to the relatively young age of the women in my sample. The 1984 census data on education of women in Tunis indicate an illiteracy rate (no schooling) of only 20.6 percent for women ages twenty to twenty-nine, versus 44 percent for women ages thirty to thirty-nine and 77 percent for women between the ages of forty and forty-nine (Tunisia I.N.S. 1984, ser. 1, v. 1). Furthermore, illiteracy had dropped by 15 percent nationally between the 1984 and 1994 censuses, the period during which my research was undertaken (Institut National de la Statistique 1999).

In my survey 19.4 percent of the women had no schooling, whereas 27.8 percent had studied up to the sixth grade, 14 percent had some vocational secondary schooling such as certification in sewing, 31 percent had some high school, and 8 percent had a university-level education.

These higher-education levels may also be a function of the middle- and working-class status of the women in my survey. On the average, the households in this survey owned more high-status luxury goods than do Tunisian households in general. Ownership of luxury goods for households in the survey paralleled the patterns of two working-middle-class areas in Tunis: Bab Bhar (essentially the downtown area of the *villeneuve*) and the suburb Le Bardo.

The observation that women in my sample generally belonged to the middle and working classes is further confirmed by two classification interviews I conducted after the survey.[1] In these interviews, I asked two separate women to sort the surveys into social levels (*niveaux sociaux*) on the basis of a summary sheet describing the couple's education levels, work, income, and ownership of luxury goods. After sorting the surveys, one woman, Aida, commented that the people in the survey were all "in the middle" (*fee moutawasit*), while Zohra Belhedi, the other woman who sorted the surveys, noted that I had not included the very poor (with no income) or the extremely wealthy.

A comparison of my survey sample to general demographic characteristics of women and families in Tunis suggests that women in my sample are not significantly different from the general Tunis population, conforming almost exactly to the typical profile of two working- and middle-class neighborhoods of Tunis: Bab Bhar and the suburb Le Bardo.

Statistics for this survey have been calculated using the Systat statistical package. Although the sample size is inappropriate for using descriptive statistics to generalize about the general Tunis population, the survey's detailed, replicable, and comparable data are sufficient and applicable to most inferential statistical analyses. With the exception of chi squares, statistics (such as *t*-tests, ANOVA, and regressions), which evaluate the *relationships between variables* in a sample, are generally robust for testing whether certain statistical patterns are likely to occur by chance, even within small sample sizes. In general, chi square results are reported here only to indicate trends.[2]

In summary, this study focuses on middle- and working-class women who are married, with their children living at home. The majority of the women are first- and second-generation migrants to Tunis, with an average of six years of schooling. About one-quarter of the women work outside the home, and another 20 percent hold jobs in the informal sector, running businesses from their homes.

Notes

1. This focus on women with middle- and working-class incomes is probably an artifact of conducting interviews on the beach: The extremely well-to-do had fled Tunis for their summer vacation homes; the extremely poor could not even afford the minimal bus fare to go to the beach.
2. To correct for sample size, in addition to Pearson chi squares, I have also calculated the statistical probabilities using the Fisher exact test and the Yates corrected chi square, where appropriate.

Appendix 2: Tables

TABLE A2.1 Mean Number of Households (HHs) Tunisian Women Visit According to Network Type

Type of Network	N	Mean HHs[a] Kin	Mean HHs[a] Neighbors	Mean HHs[a] Friends	Mean HHs[a] Total
Exclusive kin	13	11.5	0.6	0.2	11.9
Neighbor	13	12.0	5.7	0.2	18.0
Friend	8	14.4	0.9	7.3+[c]	21.8+[c]
Total[b]	34[b]	12.2	2.5	1.7+[c]	16.6+
Network composition compared (p <)		.362[d]	.000[d]	.000[d]	.005[d]

NOTES

[a] These numbers reflect households (HHs), not total number of people the woman visits, which would be significantly higher.

[b] Two surveys did not have complete network data.

[c] Because exact number of friends were difficult to obtain for women with group friendship patterns, only the specific friends women mentioned by name are included. Hence these figures are underestimates.

[d] Based on ANOVA. Differences between networks on number of friends and neighbors is an artifact of my categorization: Networks were considered kin exclusive networks if total friends and neighbors were less than two; neighbor networks if there were at least three neighbors in the network; friendship networks if there were at least three friends. Statistics are given here only to illustrate the robustness of categories.

TABLE A2.2   Tunisian Women's Network and Demographic Characteristics Compared

Type of Network	N	Percentage Migrant Women	Percentage > 6th Grade	Percentage Now Employed	Mean Income (D/mo)
Exclusive kin	13	54	46.2	30.8	184.7
Neighbor	13	83.3	38.5	0.0	157.9
Friend	8	50	87.5	50.0	345.6
Total survey	36	65	52.8	22.2	216.5
Relationship between network type and demographic factors (p <)		.20 [a]	.02 [b]	.02 [a]	.000 [b]

NOTES

[a] From chi squares. Given the small n in the sample, chi square calculations are provided only to suggest trends.

[b] based on ANOVA tests

TABLE A2.3   Tunisian Women's Networks, Marriage, and Residence Practices
Compared

Type of Network	*N*	*Percentage Live with Kin*	*Percentage Endogamy*	*Percentage Arranged Marriage*	*Percentage Regional Endgamy*
Exclusive kin	13	61.5	61.5	15.4	84.6
Neighbor	13	53.8	61.5	30.8	69.2
Friend	8	0	14.4	14.3	14.3
Total survey [a]	35	44.1	54.3	22.9	65.7
Chi square [b] (p <)		.028	.085	.556	.007

NOTES

(a) One single woman excluded from tabulations.

(b) Given the small sample size, chi squares are provided as indications of possible tendencies only.

TABLE A2.4   Statistical Relations Between Tunisian Women's Demographic and Network
Characteristics

Demographic Characteristics	Migration	Endogamy	Size of Network	No. of Kin in Network	No. of Neighbors in Network	No. of Friends in Network
Household income	p< .821[a]	p< .229[b]	p< .000[c]	p< .000[c]	p< .005[c]	p< .000[c]
Women's education	p< .083[a]	p< .046[1b]	p< .000[c]	p< .000[c]	p< .011[c]	p< .001[c]
Migration	NA	p< .052[d]	p< .181[a]	p< .037[2a]	p< .206[a]	p< .206[a]

NOTES

1. This relation is inverse. The higher the woman's education, the less likely she is to marry a relative.
2. This relation is inverse. A migrant woman is likely to have fewer kin in her network.
a. Based on *t*-test
b. Based on ANOVA
c. Based on regression
d. Based on chi square

Glossary

'Eed essgheer—Holiday breaking the Ramadan fast

'Eed ('Eedet)—Religious holiday(s)

'Eed ekkabeer—Feast of the slaughter of a sheep

Affines—In-laws; relatives through marriage

Bac—High school completion exam needed to enter a university

Bilateral kinship—Kinship that is reckoned through both the male and female line

Bridewealth—Money or goods paid to the bride and/or her family by the groom and his kin to establish a marriage

Consanguineal kin—Kin related by "blood"; biological kin

Couscous—Tunisian national dish made of semolina

Denotive kinship terminology—A system of naming relatives that distinguishes each specific individual by his or her relationship to the person speaking

Dowry—Goods brought to the marriage by the bride and/or her family

Endogamy—Marriage within the group

Fetiha—Engagement party at which a *soura* is read from the Koran

Fictive kin—Kin who have no biological relationship, but who believe or consider themselves to be from the same kin group

Fitra elkhutouba—Engagement period

Hafla (Haflet)—Celebration(s) or large party(ies)

Hajj—The pilgrimage to Mecca; one of the duties enjoined on all Muslims who are able to perform it

Hammam—Turkish steam bath

Henna—A red dye used to stain the feet and hands

Hijab—A revivalist form of veiling that has arisen in the past few decades in the Middle East in which the woman wears a tight head covering, similar to a nun's wimple, with a typically tailored European-style long dress or skirt

Jaleba—Long traditional woman's robe

Khutouba—Engagement, betrothal

Mabrouk—Congratulations

Mahr—Bridewealth

Matrilineal descent—Descent traced through the female line

Medina—Old Arab section of a city

Mlek—Party celebrating the signing of the wedding contract

Moulid—Holiday celebrating the birth of the Prophet

Mounesiba (Mounesibet)—Social occasion(s) or social event(s)

Mousim—Literally "season"; period when gifts are given on specific holidays to the future bride

Parallel cousin—A child related to the speaker through same-sex siblings (father's brother's child or mother's sister's child)

Patron-client relations—An unequal but socially established relationship of service by a lower-status person or group (client) to a higher-status person or group (patron) who provides special privileges to the client such as land use, protection, or economic assistance

Patrilineal descent—Descent traced through the male line

Patrilocal residence—Residence of a married couple with the husband's kin

Ramadan—Religious month of fasting in Islam from sunup to sundown

Quran—The holy text of Islam, received by the Prophet Muhammed

Sdeq—Marriage contract

Sifsaree—Traditional Tunisian covering for women; a white sheet that women throw on over their everyday clothing, like a coat, when leaving the house

Sixième—High school qualifying exam after completion of sixth grade

Souk—Market

Soura—Verse from the Quran

Tahour—Circumcision

Waqt elwuleda—Accouchement, time of the birth of a child

Youm elkhutouba—Betrothal day, when the husband's family first proposes marriage to the girl's family

Zeeara (Zeearat)—Visit(s)

Zhez—Bride's trousseau or dowry

Glossary of Tunisian Kinship Terms

Tunisian kinship terminology can be classified as a modified Sudanese pattern. This denotive system is highly descriptive, using a specific term for almost every individual member of the kinship group.[1] This system has the advantage of easily delineating the exact nature of the link between people, and in particular, specifying whether the relative is related patrilineally (through one's father) or matrilineally (through the mother). Thus, for example, one's paternal uncle is termed *'am* (literally father's brother), whereas one's maternal uncle is referred to as one's *khal* (mother's brother). A person's paternal aunt would be the *'ama* (father's sister), but an aunt by marriage to one's paternal uncle would be a *mart 'ama* (literally wife of my father's brother). The glossary below defines the most common kinship terms in this study.

'Amm ('Amoum)—Paternal uncle(s) (father's brother)
'Amma ('Ammet)—Paternal aunt(s) (father's sister)
'Azeez—Grandfather, sometimes also called *jid*
'Azeeza—Grandmother, sometimes also called *jidda*
Bint (Bnet)—Daughter(s)
Bint 'amm—Paternal cousin (father's brother's daughter)
Bint 'amma—Paternal cousin (father's sister's daughter)
Bint khal—Maternal cousin (mother's brother's daughter)
Bint khala—Maternal cousin (mother's sister's daughter)
Bou—Father

Hmet—Mother-in-law
Hmou—Father-in-law
Khal (Khouel)—Maternal uncle(s) (mother's brother)
Khala (Khalet)—Maternal aunt(s) (mother's sister)
Khateeb—Fiancé
Khateeba—Fiancée
Khou—Brother
Louza—Sister in-law; also called *mart khou*—brother's wife
Mart—Wife
Mart ʿam—Aunt (father's brother's wife)
Mart khal—Aunt (mother's brother's wife)
Nseeb—Male in-law or unspecified distant male relative
Nseeba—Female in-law or unspecified distant female relative
Rajil—Husband
Rajil ʿamma—Uncle (father's sister's husband)
Rajil ukht—Brother-in-law (sister's husband)
Rajil khala—Uncle (mother's sister's husband)
Silf—Brother-in-law: the brother of a woman's husband
Silfa—Sister-in-law: the sister of a woman's husband
Ukht—Sister
Um—Mother
Wild (Wled)—Son(s)
Wild ʿamm—Paternal cousin (father's brother's son)
Wild ʿamma—Paternal cousin (father's sister's son)
Wild khal—Maternal cousin (mother's brother's son)
Wild khala—Maternal cousin (mother's sister's son)

Notes

1. Tunisians do lump together some in-laws and distant kin whose relationship is unclear into the term *nseeb*. Frequently fictive kin fit into this vague category.

Suggestions for Further Reading

The past few decades have seen an explosion in the literature on women and the family in the Middle East. I offer here some suggestions to guide further research. For readers interested in the gendered use of space in the Middle East, Lila Abu Lughod's article "A Community of Secrets: The Separate World of Bedouin Women," *Signs* 10, no. 4 (1985): 637–657, provides an insightful analysis of the issues. For a historical background on Muslim women's roles, readers may want to consult Leila Ahmed's *Women and Gender in Islam* (New Haven, Conn.: Yale University Press, 1992), and Nikki Keddie and Beth Baron's *Women in Middle Eastern History* (New Haven, Conn.: Yale University Press, 1991). An excellent introduction to research on women and development in the Middle East is Valentine Moghadam's *Modernizing Women: Gender and Social Change in the Middle East* (Boulder, Colo.: Lynne Rienner, 1993). Homa Hoodfar's *Between Marriage and the Market: Intimate Politics and Survival in Cairo* (Berkeley: University of California Press, 1997) is one of the few studies to explore women's survival strategies in the Middle East; for Latin American research on the subject, one should start with Sylvia Chant's *Women and Survival in Mexican Cities* (Manchester, England: Manchester University Press, 1991). Readers interested in Middle Eastern women's roles in the informal economy should consult Richard Lobban's *Middle Eastern Women and the Invisible Economy* (Gainesville: University Press of Florida, 1998a). Finally, Laurie Brand's *Women, the State and Political Liberalization: Middle Eastern and North African Experiences* (New York: Columbia University Press, 1998) offers a detailed analysis of the political and social changes affecting women in the region.

Bibliography

ABC News, 1999. http://www.abcnews.go.com/reference/countries/TS.html.

Abdel Kefi, J. 1987. La réponse de l'Etat au processus d'urbanisation. In *Tunisie au présent: Une modernité au-dessus de tout soupçon?*, edited by M. Camau and J. Abdel Kefi. Paris: Editions du centre national de la récherche scientifique.

Abu Lughod, L. 1993. *Writing women's worlds: Bedouin stories.* Berkeley: University of California Press.

_____. 1990. The romance of resistance: Tracing transformations of power through Bedouin women. *American Ethnologist* 17: 41–55.

_____. 1986. *Veiled sentiments: Honor and poetry in a Bedouin society.* Los Angeles: University of California Press.

_____. 1985. A community of secrets: The separate world of Bedouin women. *Signs* 10(4): 637–657.

Adel, F. 1996. Formation du lieu conjugal et nouveaux modèles familiaux en Algerie. In *Femmes, culture et société au Maghreb*, edited by R. Bourquia, M. Charrad, and N. Gallagher, v. 1: 139–155. Casablanca: Afrique-Orient.

Agarwal, B. 1991. Social security and the family: Coping with seasonality and calamity in rural India. In *Social security in developing countries*, edited by E. Ahmad, J. Dreze, J. Hills, and A. Sen, pp. 171–244. Oxford: Clarendon Press.

Ahmed, L. 1992. *Women and gender in Islam: Historical roots of a modern debate.* New Haven, Conn.: Yale University Press.

Altorki, S. 1986. *Women in Saudi Arabia: Ideology and behavior among the elite.* New York: Columbia University Press.

_____. 1977. Family organization and women's power in urban Saudi Arabian society. *Journal of Anthropological Research* 33: 277–287.

Altorki, S., and C. F. El Solh. 1988. *Arab women in the field: Studying your own society*. Syracuse, N.Y.: Syracuse University Press.

Amin, Sajeda. 1998. Family structure and change in rural Bangladesh. *Population Studies* 52: 201–213.

Asfaruddin, A., ed. 1999. *Hermeneutics and honor: Negotiating female "public" space in Islamic/ate societies*. Cambridge, Mass.: Harvard Middle Eastern Monographs XXXII.

Aswad, B. C. 1978. Women, class and power: Examples from Hatay, Turkey. In *Women in the Muslim world*, edited by L. Beck and N. Keddie, pp. 473–481. Cambridge, Mass.: Harvard University Press.

———. 1974. Visiting patterns among women of the elite in a small Turkish city. *Anthropological Quarterly* 47(1): 9–27.

Atiya, N. 1982. *Khul-khaal: Five Egyptian women tell their stories*. Syracuse, N.Y.: Syracuse University Press.

Balaghi, S., and F. Muge Gocek. 1994. *Reconstructing gender in the Middle East*. New York: Columbia University Press.

Barakat, H. 1993. *The Arab world: Society, culture and state*. Berkeley: University of California Press.

———. 1988. The Arab family and the challenge of social transformation. In *Women and the family in the Middle East*, edited by E. W. Fernea, pp. 27–48. Austin: University of Texas Press.

Baron, B. 1989. Unveiling in early twentieth-century Egypt: Practical and symbolic considerations. *Middle Eastern Studies* 25(3): 370–386.

Belkadi-Maaouia, A., A. al-Amouri, T. al-Amouri, A. Maaouia, A. Majerti, and M. Zamih. 1981. *L'image de la femme dans la société tunisienne*. Tunis: Union Nationale des Femmes de Tunisie, Institut el-Amouri de Psychologie Appliquée.

Ben Abdelkader, R., A. Abdeljelil, and A. Naour. 1977. *Peace Corps English Tunisian Arabic dictionary*. Washington, D.C.: U.S. Government-Peace Corps.

Benedict, P. 1974. The Kabul Günü: Structured visiting in an Anatolian town. *Anthropological Quarterly* 47(1): 28–48.

Ben Salem, L. 1967. La mobilité sociale et ses incidences sur la famille. *Revue Tunisienne de Sciences Sociales* 4(11): 37–47.

Bernard, C. 1990. Les femmes salariés et non salariées au Maghreb, des travailleuses à plein temps et——hors du temps. In *Femmes du Maghreb au présent: Le dot, le travail, l'identité*, edited by M. Gadant and M. Kasriel, pp. 89–140. Paris: C.N.R.S.

Berry-Chikahoui, I. 1998. The invisible economy at the edges of the medina of Tunis. In *Middle Eastern women and the invisible economy*, edited by R. Lobban, pp. 215–233. Gainesville: University Press of Florida.

Betteridge, A. E. 1985. Gift exchange in Iran: The locus of self-identity in social interaction. *Anthropological Quarterly* 58(4): 190–202.

Boserup, E. 1990. Economic change and the roles of women. In *Persistent inequalities: Women and world development*, edited by I. Tinker, pp. 14–24. Oxford: Oxford University Press.

_____. 1976. *Women's role in economic development*. London: Allen and Unwin.

Bott, E. 1971. *Family and social network: Rules, norms and external relationships in ordinary urban families*. 2d ed. New York: The Free Press.

Boucebci, M. 1989. Filiation, identité et roles sociaux dans un monde en changement. *Femmes et pouvoir: Peuples méditerraneéns* 48–49: 107–112.

Bouraoui, A. 1986. Les mariages préférentiels. Paper presented at Les relations interpersonnelles dans la famille magrebrebine. Colloquium held by C.E.R.E.S. in Tunis 27–30 October 1986 (photocopied).

Bourquia, R., M. Charrad, and N. Gallagher, eds. 1996. *Femmes, cultures et société au maghreb*. Casablanca: Afrique Orient.

Brand, L. A. 1998. *Women, the state and political liberalization: Middle Eastern and North African experiences*. New York: Columbia University Press.

Camilleri, C. 1973. *Jeunesse, famille et développement: Essai sur le changement socio-culturel dans un pays du tiers-monde (Tunisie)*. Paris: Centre National de la Recherche Scientifique.

Caplow, T. 1982. Christmas gifts and kin networks. *American Sociological Review* 47(3): 383–392.

Chamari, A. C. 1990. Femmes et loi en Tunisie. Paper presented to WIDER, Tunis.

Chant, S. 1991. *Women and survival in Mexican cities: Perspectives on gender, labour markets and low-income households*. Manchester, England: Manchester University Press.

Charrad, M. 2001. State and gender in the Maghrib. In *Women and power in the Middle East*, edited by S. Joseph and S. Slymovics, pp. 61–71. Philadelphia: University of Pennsylvania Press.

_____. 1998. Cultural diversity within Islam: Veils and laws in Tunisia. In *Women in Muslim societies: Diversity within unity*, edited by H. L. Bodman and N. Tohidi, pp. 63–79. Boulder, Colo.: Lynne Rienner.

_____. 1996. State and gender in the Maghrib. In *Arab women: Between defiance and restraint*, edited by S. Sabbagh, pp. 221–228. New York: Interlink Publishing.

Cheal, D. 1988. *The gift economy*. London: Routledge.

Climo, J. 1992. *Distant parents*. New Brunswick, N.J.: Rutgers University Press.

Collier, J. F., and S. J. Yanagisako. 1987. *Gender and kinship: Essays toward a unified analysis*. Stanford, Calif.: Stanford University Press.

Cuisenier, J. 1960. Structures parentales et structures vicinales en Tunisie. *IBLA* 23: 401–426.

Dachmi, A. 1997. La survalorisation de l'émigré au détriment de l'image paternelle dans le milieu traditionnel marocain. In *Migration internationale et changement sociaux dans le Maghreb*, edited by A. Bencherifa, L. Michalak, H. Mzabi, and G. Sabagh, pp. 149–158. Tunis: Université de Tunis.

Davis, D. A., and S. S. Davis. 1993. Dilemmas of adolescence: Courtship, sex and marriage in a Moroccan town. In *Everyday life in the Muslim Middle East*, edited by D. L. Bowen and E. A. Early, pp. 84–90. Bloomington: Indiana University Press.

Davis, S. S. 1993. Changing gender relations in a Moroccan town. In *Arab women: Old boundaries, new frontiers*, edited by J. Tucker, pp. 208–223. Bloomington: Indiana University Press.

_____. 1983. *Patience and power: Women's lives in a Moroccan village*. Cambridge, Mass.: Schenkman Publishing Co.

Davis, S.S., and D. A. Davis. 1989. *Adolescence in a Moroccan town*. New Brunswick, N.J.: Rutgers University Press.

Delaney, C. 1991. *The seed and the soil*. Berkeley: University of California Press.

Demeerseman, A. 1967. *La famille tunisienne et les temps nouveaux*. Tunis: Maison Tunisienne de l'Edition.

Denoeux, G. 1993. *Urban unrest in the Middle East: A comparative study of informal networks in Egypt, Iran, and Lebanon*. New York: SUNY Press.

di Leonardo, M. 1987. The female world of cards and holidays: Women, families and the work of kinship. *Signs* 12(3): 440–453.

Dixon, J. 1987. Social security in the Middle East. In *Social welfare in the Middle East*, edited by J. Dixon, pp. 163–177. London: Croom Helm.

Dorsky, S. 1986. *Women of 'Amran: A Middle Eastern ethnographic study*. Salt Lake City: University of Utah Press.

Dwyer, D. 1978. *Images and self-images: Male and female in Morocco.* New York: Columbia University Press.

Early, E. 1998. Nest eggs of gold and beans: Baladi Egyptian women's invisible capital. In *Middle Eastern women and the invisible economy,* edited by R. Lobban, pp.132–147. Gainesville: University Press of Florida.

———. 1993a. *Baladi women of Cairo: Playing with an egg and a stone.* Boulder, Colo.: Lynne Rienner.

———. 1993b. Getting it together: Baladi Egyptian businesswomen. In *Arab women: Old boundaries, new frontiers,* edited by J. E. Tucker, pp. 84–101. Bloomington: Indiana University Press.

Eickelman, C. 1993. Fertility and social change in Oman: Women's perspectives. *Middle East Journal* 47(4): 652–666.

———. 1984. *Women and community in Oman.* New York: New York University Press.

Farsoun, S., and K. Farsoun. 1974. Class and patterns of association among kinsmen in contemporary Lebanon. *Anthropological Quarterly* 47(1): 93–111.

Ferchiou, S. 1998. "Invisible" work, work "at home," and the condition of women in Tunisia. In *Middle Eastern women and the invisible economy,* edited by R. Lobban, pp. 187–197. Gainesville: University Press of Florida.

———. 1996. Feminisme d'état en Tunisie: Ideologie dominante et resistance feminine. In *Femmes, culture et société au maghreb,* edited by R. Bourquia, M. Charrad, and N. Gallagher, v. II: 119–140. Casablanca: Afrique-Orient.

Fernea, E. W., ed. 1985. *Women and the family in the Middle East: New voices of change.* Austin: University of Texas Press.

———. 1975. *A street in Marrakech.* New York: Doubleday.

Friedl, E. 1991. *Women of Deh Koh: Lives in an Iranian village.* New York: Penguin Books.

Gadant, M., and M. Kasriel. 1990. *Femmes du Maghreb au présent: Le dot, le travail, l'identité.* Paris: Centre National de la Recherche Scientifique.

Galal, S. 1995. Women and development in the Maghreb countries. In *Gender and development in the Arab world: Women's economic participation, patterns and policies,* edited by N. F. Khoury and V. M. Moghadam, pp. 49–70. London: Zed Books.

Ghabra, S. N. 1987. *Palestinians in Kuwait: The family and the politics of survival.* Boulder, Colo.: Westview Press.

Ghifari, N. M. 1989. *Social security in Islam*. Lahore, Pakistan: Atiq Publishing House.

Ginat, J. 1982. *Women in Muslim rural society: Status and role in family and community*. New Brunswick, N.J.: Transaction Books.

Goffman, I. 1971. *Relations in public*. New York: Basic Books.

Gonzales de la Rocha, M. 1994. *The resources of poverty: Women and survival in a Mexican city*. Oxford: Blackwell.

Goode, W. J. 1970. *World revolution and family patterns*. New York: The Free Press.

Gottlieb, B. 1981. *Social networks and social support*. Beverly Hills, Calif.: Sage Publications.

Graham-Brown, S. 1988. *Images of women: The portrayal of women in photography of the Middle East 1860–1950*. London: Quartet Books.

Guerraoui, D. 1996. Famille et développement à Fes. In *Femmes, culture et société au maghreb*, edited by R. Bourquia, M. Charrad, and N. Gallagher, v. 1: 157–178. Casablanca: Afrique-Orient.

Hatem, M. 1999. Modernization, the state and the family in Middle East women's studies. In *Social history of women and gender in the modern Middle East*, edited by M. Meriwether and J. Tucker, pp. 63–88. Boulder, Colo.: Westview Press.

Hegland, M. E. 1991. Political roles of Aliabad women: The public-private dichotomy transcended. In *Women in Middle Eastern history*, edited by N. Keddie and B. Baron, pp. 215–232. New Haven, Conn.: Yale University Press.

Hessini, L. 1994. Wearing the hijab in contemporary Morocco: Choice and identity. In *Reconstructing gender in the Middle East*, edited by F. Göceck and S. Balaghi, pp. 40–56. New York: Columbia University Press.

Holmes-Eber, P. 1997a. L'impact de la migration sur la famille et la femme tunisienne. In *Migration internationale et changements sociaux dans le maghreb*, edited by A. Bencherifa, L. Michelak, H. Mzabi, and G. Sabagh, pp. 131–148. Tunis: Université de Tunis.

_____. 1997b. Migration, urbanization and women's kin networks in Tunis. *Journal of comparative family studies* 28(2): 54–72.

_____. 1996. On beaches and benches: Gender, space and interviewing strategies through the eyes of anthropology and Middle East studies. In *Conference on international, comparative and area studies: Integrating scholarship on the Middle East* (April 26–27). Milwaukee: University of Wisconsin.

Hoodfar, H. 1998. Women in Cairo's (in)visible economy: Linking local and national trends. In *Middle Eastern women and the invisible economy*, edited by R. Lobban, pp. 245–262. Gainesville: University Press of Florida.

———. 1997. *Between marriage and the market: Intimate politicas and survival in Cairo*. Berkeley: University of California Press.

———. 1990. Survival strategies in low-income households in Cairo. *Journal of South Asian and Middle Eastern Studies* 13(4): 22–41.

Hyde, L. 1983. *The gift: Imagination and the erotic property of life*. New York: Random House.

Institut National de la Statistique. 1999, July 1. http://www.ins.nat.tun.

Joseph, S. 1983. Working-class women's networks in a sectarian state: A political paradox. *American Ethnologist* 10(1): 1–23.

———. 1978. The neighborhood street in Lebanon. In *Women in the Muslim world*, edited by L. Beck and N. Keddie, pp. 541–558. Cambridge, Mass.: Harvard University Press.

Kanafani, A. S. 1993. Rites of hospitality and aesthetics. In *Everyday life in the Muslim Middle East*, edited by D. L. Bowen and E. A. Early, pp. 128–135. Bloomington: Indiana University Press.

———. 1983. *Aesthetics and ritual in the United Arab Emirates*. Beirut: American University of Beirut.

Karoui, N. 1982. La femme tunisienne et le phénomène "bureau": Etude sociologique sur les attitudes et conduites des jeunes femmes tunisiennes dans l'administration PTT. *Revue Tunisienne de Sciences Sociales* 70/71: 143–167.

Keddie, N., and B. Baron. 1991. *Women in Middle Eastern history: Shifting boundaries in sex and gender*. New Haven, Conn.: Yale University Press.

Kressel, G. M. 1992. *Descent through males*. Wiesbaden, Germany: Otto Harrassowitz.

Khoury, N. F., and V. Moghadam, eds. 1995. *Gender and development in the Arab world*. London: Zed Books.

Labidi, L. 1989. *Cabra Hachma: Sexualité et tradition*. Tunis: Dar Annawras.

———. 1987. Jathour elharka elnissaea bitunis. Unpublished paper, Tunis.

Larson, B. K. 1998. Women, work and the informal economy in rural Egypt. In *Middle Eastern women and the invisible economy*, edited by R. Lobban. Gainesville: University Press of Florida.

Leigh, G. K. 1982. Kinship interaction over the life span. *Journal of Marriage and the Family* 44(1): 197–208.

Lfarakh, A. 1994. Composition et structures des ménages au Maroc. Unpublished manuscript, Rabat.

Lobban, R., ed. 1998a. *Middle Eastern women and the invisible economy.* Gainesville: University Press of Florida.

_____. 1998b. Women in the invisible economy in Tunis. In *Middle Eastern women and the invisible economy,* edited by R. Lobban, pp. 198–214. Gainesville: University Press of Florida.

Lomnitz, L. A. 1977. *Networks and marginality: Life in a Mexican shantytown.* New York: Academic Press.

Mabro, J. 1991. *Veiled half-truths: Western travellers' perceptions of Middle Eastern women.* London: I. B. Tauris.

MacLeod, A. E. 1991. *Accomodating protest: Working women and the new veiling in Cairo.* New York: Columbia University Press.

Mahfoudh, D. 1990. Anciennes et nouvelles formes de travail des femmes à domicile en Tunisie. In *Femmes du Maghreb au présent: Le dot, le travail, l'identité,* edited by M. Gadant and M. Kasriel, pp. 159–172. Paris: C.N.R.S.

Mahfoudh-Draoui, D. 1993. *Paysannes de Marnissa: La difficile accès à la modernité.* Tunis: Charma Edition.

Mayer, A. E. 1995. Reform of personal status laws in North Africa: A problem of Islamic or Mediterranean laws. *Middle East Journal* 49(3): 432–446.

McCann, L. 1997. Patrilocal co-residential units (PCUs) in al-Barha: Dual household structure in a provincial town in Jordan. *Journal of Comparative Family Studies* 28(2): 113–135.

Mernissi, F. 1987a. *Beyond the veil: Male-female dynamics in modern Muslim society.* Bloomington: Indiana University Press.

_____. 1987b. *Women and Islam: An historical and theological enquiry,* translated by Mary Jo Lakeland. Oxford: Basil Blackwell.

Meriweather, M. 1999. *The kin who count: Family and society in Ottoman Aleppo.* Austin: University of Texas Press.

Metcalf, B. P., ed. 1996. *Making Muslim space in North America and Europe.* Berkeley: University of California Press.

Michael, B. 1998. Baggara women as market strategists. In *Middle Eastern women and the invisible economy,* edited by R. Lobban. Gainesville: University Press of Florida.

_____. 1997. Female heads of patriarchal households: The Baggara. *Journal of Comparative Family Studies* 18(2): 170–182.

Midgley, J. 1984. *Social security and inequality in the Third World.* Chichester, England: John Wiley & Sons.

Mitchell, J. C. 1974. Social networks. *Annual Review of Anthropology* 3: 279–299.

Moghadam, V. M. 1998. *Women, work and economic reform in the Middle East and North Africa.* Boulder, Colo.: Lynne Rienner.

———. 1993. *Modernizing women: Gender and social change in the Middle East.* Boulder, Colo.: Lynne Rienner.

Momsen, J., and V. Kinnaird, eds. 1993. *Different places, different voices: Gender and development in Africa, Asia and Latin America.* London: Routledge.

Morrison, C., and B. Talbi. 1996. *Long-term growth in Tunisia.* Paris: OECD.

Naamane-Guessous, S. 1988. *Au dela de toute pudeur: La sexualité feminine au Maroc.* Casablanca: Eddif Maroc.

Nelson, C. 1974. Public and private politics: Women in the Middle Eastern world. *American Ethnologist* 1(3): 551–563.

Netting, R. Mc., R. R. Wilk, and E. J. Arnould. 1984. *Households: Comparative and historical studies of the domestic group.* Berkeley: University of California Press.

Norris, W. P. 1985. The social networks of impoverished Brazilian women: Work patterns and household structure in an urban squatter settlement. In *Women in International Development Working Papers* #84. East Lansing: Michigan State University.

North Africa Journal. 1998, June 27. Vol. 34. http:/www.north.africa.com.

Papanek, H. 1979. Family status production: The "work" and "non-work" of women. *Signs* 4(4): 775–781.

Rapp, R. 1987. Toward a nuclear freeze? The gender politics of Euro-American kinship analysis. In *Gender and kinship: Essays toward a unified analysis,* edited by J. F. Collier and S. J. Yanagisako, pp. 119–131. Stanford, Calif.: Stanford University Press.

———. 1982. Family and class in contemporary America: Notes toward an understanding of ideology. In *Rethinking the family: Some feminist questions,* edited by B. Thorne and M. Yalom, pp. 168–224. New York: Longman.

Rassam, A. 1980. Women and domestic power in Morocco. *International Journal of Middle East Studies* 12(2): 171–179.

Rejeb, S. 1987. Le divorce d'après le veçu de femmes tunisiennes cadres. *Revue Tunisienne de Sciences Sociales* 84/87: 277–345.

_____. 1986. Destructuration, restructuration de la famille Tunisienne. *Revue Tunisienne de Sciences Sociales* 84/87: 245–299.

Republique Tunisienne. 1988. *La femme et la famille tunisienne à travers les chiffres.* Tunis: Ministere du Plan.

Rosander, E. E. 1991. *Women in a borderland: Managing Muslim identity where Morocco meets Spain.* Stockholm Studies in Social Anthropology 26. Stockholm, Sweden: Stockholm University.

Rosenthal, C. J. 1985. Kinkeeping in the familial division of labor. *Journal of Marriage and the Family* 47(4): 965–973.

Roy, P. 1984. Extended kinship ties in Malaysia. *Journal of Comparative Family Studies* 15(2): 175–193.

Royaume du Maroc. 1996. *Famille au Maroc: Les reseaux de solidarité familiale.* Rabat: Centre d'Etudes et de Récherches Demographiques.

Rugh, A. B. 1984. *Family in contemporary Egypt.* Syracuse, N.Y.: Syracuse University Press.

Safa, H. I. 1995. *The myth of the male breadwinner: Women and industrialization in the Caribbean.* Boulder, Colo.: Westview Press.

Sage, C. 1993. Deconstructing the household: Women's roles under commodity relations in highland Bolivia. In *Different places, different voices: Gender and development in Africa, Asia and Latin America*, edited by J. H. Momsen and V. Kinnaird, pp. 243–256. London: Routledge.

Sahli, S. 1981. Le couple entre l'union et la rupture. *Revue Tunisienne de Sciences Sociales* 18(66): 117–130.

Salman, M., H. Kazi, N. Yuva-Davis, L. al-Hamdani, S. Botman, and D. Lehrman. 1987. *Women in the Middle East.* London: Zed Books.

Samuelson, R. J. 1990. *Book of vital world statistics.* London: Hutchison Business Books.

Segalen, M. 1984. Nuclear is not independent: Organization of the household in the Pays Bigouden Sud in the nineteenth and twentieth centuries. In *Households: Comparative and historical studies of the domestic group*, edited by R. Netting, R. Wilk, and E. Arnould, pp. 163–186. Berkeley: University of California Press.

Shaaban, B. 1988. *Both right and left handed: Arab women talk about their lives.* London: Women's Press Limited.

Shami, S. 1997. Domesticity reconfigured: Women in squatter areas of Amman. In *Organizing women: Formal and informal women's groups in the Middle East*, edited by Dawn Chatty and Annika Rabo. Oxford: Berg.

———. 1988. Studying your own: The complexities of a shared culture. In *Arab women in the field: Studying your own society*, edited by S. Altorki and C. F. El Solh, pp. 115–138. Syracuse, N.Y.: Syracuse University Press.

Shukri, S. 1999. *Social changes and women in the Middle East: State policy, education, economics and development*. Aldreshot, England: Ashgate.

Signoles, P., A. Belhedi, J. Miossec, and H. Dlala. 1980. *Tunis: Evolution et fonctionnement de l'éspace urbain*. Centre interuniversitaire d'études méditerranéenes et Equipe du recherche associeé, No. 76. Tours: C.N.R.S.

Singerman, D. 1998. Engaging informality: Women, work and politics in Cairo. In *Middle Eastern women and the invisible economy*, edited by R. Lobban. Gainesville: University Press of Florida.

———. 1996. The family and community as politics: The popular sector in Cairo. In *Development, change and gender in Cairo: A view from the household*, edited by D. Singerman and H. Hoodfar. Bloomington: Indiana University Press.

———. 1995. *Avenues of participation: Family politics and networks in urban quarters of Cairo*. Princeton, N.J.: Princeton University Press.

———. 1994. Where has all the power gone? Women and politics in popular quarters of Cairo. In *Reconstructing gender in the Middle East*, edited by F. Göçek and S. Balaghi, pp. 174–200. New York: Columbia University Press.

Sraieb, N. 1974. Mutations socio-économiques de la famille en Tunisie. *Revue Algerienne des Sciences Juridiques, Economiques et Politiques* 11(3): 127–132.

Stack, C. B. 1974. *All our kin: Strategies for survival in a black community*. New York: Harper & Row.

Stevenson, T. 1997. Migration, family and household in highland Yemen: The impact of socio-economic and political change and cultural ideas on domestic organization. *Journal of Comparative Family Studies* 28(2): 14–53.

Taamallah, L. 1982. Les femmes et l'emploi en Tunisie. *Revue Tunisienne de Sciences Sociales* 70/71: 143–166.

———. 1981. La scolarisation et la formation professionnelle des femmes en Tunisie. *Revue Tunisienne de Sciences Sociales* 68/69: 107–127.

Taamallah, M. 1990. Les femmes, les motivations au travail et l'insertion dans la vie active en Tunisie. In *Femmes du Maghreb au présent: Le dot, le travail, l'identité*, edited by M. Gadant and M. Kasriel, pp. 141–158. Paris: C.N.R.S.

———. 1986. L'urbanisation: Ses consequences sur les structures socio-démographiques en Tunisie. *Revue Tunisienne de Sciences Sociales* 84/87: 377–396.

Tapper, N. 1991. *Bartered brides: Politics, gender and marriage in an Afghan tribal society*. Cambridge, England: Cambridge University Press.

———. 1983. Gender and religion in a Turkish town: A comparison of two types of formal women's gatherings. In *Women's religious experience: Cross-cultural perspectives*, edited by P. Holden, pp. 71–87. London: Croom Helm.

Tessler, M., J. Rogers, and D. Schneider. 1978. Women's emancipation in Tunisia. In *Women in the Muslim world*, edited by L. Beck and N. Keddie, pp. 141–158. Cambridge, Mass.: Harvard University Press.

Thorne, B. 1982. Feminist rethinking of the family: An overview. In *Rethinking the family: Some feminist questions*, edited by B. Thorne and M. Yalom, pp. 1–24. New York: Longman.

Tucker, J. 1993. The Arab family in history: Otherness and the study of the family. In *Arab women: Old boundaries, new frontiers*, edited by J. E. Tucker, pp. 195–207. Bloomington: Indiana University Press.

Tunisia Digest. 1993. Vol. 2(1). Washington, D.C.: Tunisian Information Office.

Tunisia Digest. 1992. Vol. 1(4). Washington, D.C.: Tunisian Information Office.

Tunisia I.N.S. (Institut National de la Statistique). 1984. *Rencensement général de la population et de l'habitat*. Tunis: I.N.S.

Uhl, S. 1991. Forbidden friends: Cultural veils of female friendship in Andalusia. *American Ethnologist* 18(1): 90–105.

Webber, S. 1991. *Romancing the real: Folklore and ethnographic representation in North Africa*. Philadelphia: University of Pennsylvania Press.

Wier, S. 1985. *Qat in Yemen: Consumption and social change*. London: British Museum.

Wiesner, M. E. 1993. *Women and gender in early modern Europe*. Cambridge: Cambridge University Press.

White, J. 1994. *Money makes us relatives: Women's labor in urban Turkey*. Austin: University of Texas Press.

Wikan, U. 1982. *Behind the veil in Arabia: Women in Oman*. Chicago: University of Chicago Press.

_____. 1980. *Life among the poor in Cairo*. Translated by A. Henning. New York: Tavistock Publications.

Wilson, T. D. 1998. Weak ties, strong ties: Network principles in Mexican migration. *Human Organization* 57(4): 394–403.

_____. 1990. Reciprocity networks in anthropological research. *Society for Economic Anthropology Newsletter* 10(10): 11–18.

Yanagisako, S. J. 1979. Family and household: The analysis of domestic groups. In *Annual review of anthropology*, edited by B. J. Siegel, A. R. Beals, and S. A. Tyler, v. 8: 161–205. Palo Alto, Calif.: Annual Reviews, Inc.

Young, M., and P. Wilmott. 1957. *Family and kinship in East London*. Glencoe, Ill.: The Free Press.

Young, W., and S. Shami. 1997. Anthropological approaches to the Arab family: An introduction. *Journal of Comparative Family Studies* 28(2): 1–14.

Zamiti-Horchani, M. 1997. Les épouse des travailleurs migrants demeurées au pays: Chefs de ménages ou substitus des absents. In *Migration internationale et changements sociaux dans le magheb*, edited by A. Bencherifa, L. Michelak, H. Mzabi, and G. Sabagh, pp. 159–180. Tunis: Université de Tunis.

_____. 1986. Tunisian women, their rights and their ideas about these rights. In *Women of the Mediterranean*, edited by M. Gadant, translated by A. M. Berrett, pp. 110–119. London: Zed Books.

Zouari-Bouattour. 1996. Femme et emploi en Tunisie. In *Femmes, culture et société au maghreb*, edited by R. Bourquia, M. Charrad, and N. Gallagher, v. II: 161–182. Casablanca: Afrique-Orient.

Index